THE
TENNESSEE OUTDOORSMEN
—COOKBOOK—

THE
TENNESSEE OUTDOORSMEN
—COOKBOOK—

Jimmy Holt
and
Vernon Summerlin

Rutledge Hill Press®
Nashville, Tennessee

A Division of Thomas Nelson, Inc.
www.ThomasNelson.com

Copyright © 2002 by Jimmy Holt and Vernon Summerlin.

Published by Rutledge Hill Press, a division of Thomas Nelson, Inc., P.O. Box 141000, Nashville, Tennessee 37214.

Text illustrations by Walter Petrie.

Library of Congress Cataloging-in-Publication Data

Holt, Jimmy.
    Tennessee outdoorsmen cookbook / Jimmy Holt and Vernon Summerlin.
      p. cm.
    Includes index.
    ISBN 978-1-55853-962-4
    1. Cookery (Game) 2. Cookery (Fish) I. Summerlin, Vernon, 1943– II. Title.
TX751 .H65 2002
641.6'91—dc21
                                                            2001006632

Printed in the United States of America

02 03 04 05 06 — 5 4 3 2 1

Contents

Preface

I began to enjoy cooking about 15 years ago, and almost every day I get an urge to cook up something different. For me, cooking is fun. I guess it's like building something. When I try a new recipe and my friends tell me how tasty it is, then I know I've succeeded in something I love to do.

For more years than I can recall, I have collected recipes. As the host of *The Tennessee Outdoorsmen* television show, I receive fish and game recipes from people in all walks of life, including fine chefs, throughout Tennessee and the surrounding states. My intention when I began collecting was to publish a cookbook, but my procrastination never faltered.

Fortunately, Vernon Summerlin, who worked as a field host on my show for a few years, agreed to collaborate with me on this cookbook. Vern has his own files of recipes, saved from the recipe column he wrote when he was editor of *Tennessee Angler* magazine. And we both have favorite recipes that we've gathered from family and friends. For this book, we've selected the best from our collections.

Many recipes don't give credit to their originator because they were unsigned. And unfortunately, over the years of saving these recipes, some names were separated from recipes. If you see your recipe without a credit, we apologize and ask that you let us know so that we can give credit where credit is due in the next edition.

Over the years, Vern and I have tried most of these recipes to make sure they taste good. And we know that the many recipes sent in by hunters, fishermen, and their wives have been tried and tested many times. Most of the recipes in this book are simple to prepare—catching or hunting some of the ingredients may be the most difficult part!

We don't have a lot of beaver, bear, raccoon, and opossum recipes, but we've included enough so that you can prepare these critters if you shoot or trap them. We concentrated on fish and venison and other game common to Tennessee—and easier to come by.

Many people, including some hunters, profess that they do not like to eat wild game. "It's strong," they say. "It has a wild flavor." So it is often wasted. If you are a hunter or your spouse is, and you're both frustrated because you have never cooked wild game that satisfies your taste buds, I hope this cookbook will help you understand that the wild game that roam the woods of Tennessee and the fish that swim in our waters are delicious. Just try these recipes. This book could open a whole new world of fine food for you. However, remember that wild game has to be properly prepared, meaning cleaned correctly and washed thoroughly. So do fish and fowl.

To accompany the recipes, we've included some of our favorite stories, including one that explains why I always close my show with the advice to "wear your life jacket." We've also sprinkled fishing and hunting tips throughout the book.

I know from all the recipes in this book that hunters want to eat the game they take and fishermen want to eat their catch. Everybody wants to improve upon their own recipes or try someone else's. We know you'll find numerous dishes you'll enjoy and make a part of your cooking repertoire. Feel free to experiment with recipes by changing the seasonings to suit your tastes. Keep in mind that although we include the number of servings at the end of each recipe, the recipe may not go as far with hungry Tennessee outdoorsmen.

Speaking of the outdoors makes me think about fishing. The bluegill and shellcracker are hitting great on Old Hickory Lake. I've got to go . . .

—Jimmy Holt

THE
TENNESSEE OUTDOORSMEN
—COOKBOOK—

Chapter 1

Finny Feasts

General Fish Recipes, Catfish, Crappie, Trout, True Bass, Black Bass, Bream, Sauger/Walleye, Gar

— COOKING OUTDOORS —

Americans, from the pilgrims and wagon train pioneers to the cowboys and mountain men, have had a continuing love affair with the outdoors, and still do today. They have a real fondness for cooking and eating outdoors.

Cooking something as simple as a hot dog or as complex as an entire meal is great fun outdoors, and for some unknown reason the food tastes better.

I have cooked on an open fire—I love it—and, of course, the charcoal grill. There is a wide variety of grills available, from small hibachis to large built-in types. Covered kettles, smokers, and grills fired by gas or electricity can greatly increase and enhance the scope of your cookout style. All of these cookers work differently, and you should be familiar with the strengths and limitations of them in order to cook well.

For some real barbecue fun, take a grill and place dry gravel or crushed rock on the bottom of the firebox. This protects the grill, evenly distributes the heat, and helps prevent flame-ups from drippings. Use a generous amount of briquettes made from maple, birch, oak, elm, or other hardwoods and start the fire early enough to get a sufficiently hot bed of coals—about 30 to 40 minutes before cooking.

— PREPARING AND STORING FISH —

Fish are extremely perishable. Fish that do not have red gills, clear eyes, and a fresh odor should be thrown away. Here are a few tips for proper care:

- Keep your fish alive: Most fishing boats have aerated live wells in which fish are kept alive during the fishing day. Check your catch often and remove the dead fish and place them on ice immediately.

- Keep your fish cold: Cleaning the fish before putting them on ice is best. When placing the fish on ice, do not put them on the bottom where water collects, because water aids in deterioration.

- Cleaning and cooking your fish within two hours after catching it provides the best flavor.

- You can either fillet your catch or field dress it by removing its entrails and head, including the gills. If you prefer to scale your fish, use a fish scaler, dull knife, or a spoon. Wet the fish and scrape off the scales from tail to head.

- Filleting fish and leaving no bones is the most popular method of preparation. Most of the flesh can be cut from the bones without touching the intestines. A sharp knife is essential, and the length of the blade should fit the size of your fish. A wooden fillet board with a clip on one end is useful for holding fish. If you are outdoors, fillet your fish on a paddle, the lid of a cooler, or the gunwale.

- Treat fish with ascorbic acid to extend their freezer life by three months. Mix 2 tablespoons ascorbic acid (available in drug stores) and 1 quart water, place fish in the mixture for 20 seconds, and then double wrap and freeze immediately.

- To prepare fish for storage, wipe fillets or whole fish with a paper towel, rinse in cold water, and wrap in aluminum foil or plastic wrap before freezing or chilling.

- When storing fish, the colder the storage temperature, the longer the fish will maintain its flavor. A properly cleaned fish can be refrigerated for 24 hours with little loss of taste. Fish stored on crushed ice will remain fresh for three days, but they must not be in any water. Super-chilled fish can be kept up to a week. If you're carrying your fish a long distance, add a layer of ice and a layer of rock salt, and place wrapped fish between each layer of ice.

- Never thaw fish at room temperature; bacteria begin to flourish as the fish warm. If the fish are frozen in a block of ice, melt the ice under cold water. Place the fish on paper towels and cover with plastic wrap to finish thawing in your refrigerator.

— AVERAGE CALORIES FOR SEVERAL SPECIES —

Lean fish have fewer calories than oily ones. Vegetable oil, butter, margarine, and sauces add extra calories. Poaching and steaming are the only cooking methods in which no calories are added. Here is a guide to the average number of calories per 4-ounce serving of uncooked fish:

Bullhead	96	Salmon	223 to 254
Catfish	118	Striped bass	120
Black bass (lean)	119	Trout (small)	115
Muskellunge	125	Trout (large)	223
Northern pike	101	Walleye	106
Panfish	104	White bass	112

— COOKING FISH ON THE GRILL —

Personally, I prefer fried fish; however, cooking fish on the grill is fun and easy with few cleanup chores. Besides, fish always seems to taste better when cooked outdoors.

Place charcoal briquettes in a "pyramid shape," commonly called a pile. Light them at least 30 minutes before cooking time. When the briquettes turn ashen gray, they are ready for cooking.

Push the briquettes into a ring roughly the shape of the fish. Tossing moist hickory or apple wood chips onto the coals adds a smoky flavor to the fish, a taste which I really like.

To prepare fish fillets for grilling, dry them with a paper towel and brush with oil. Lean fish can be marinated in Italian dressing before cooking. Spread the coals and brush the grill with oil or spray it with a nonstick coating. Place the fillets skin down on the grill, or place skinless fillets on foil cut to size. An oiled grill basket is helpful for easy turning. I like to baste the fish every two minutes with lemon-butter or a marinade such as Italian dressing. Lean fish needs to be basted often, because it dries out quickly. Test the fish often, because it cooks rapidly.

— COOKING FISH OVER AN OPEN FIRE —

I like fish cooked over an open fire. It's delicious, but it's easily overcooked when the fire is too hot. Fishermen whom I've talked with over the years that enjoy open-fire cooking tell me you need to keep the fire small and the heat under control. The best woods for open-fire cooking are maple, birch, apple, hickory, beech, and other hardwoods. They burn well and give a pleasant flavor. I'm told softwoods such as pine, spruce, and hemlock cause an unpleasant flavor.

Preparing fish for open-fire cooking is easy, because you cook the whole fish with the head and tail intact to help seal in the juices. Keeping the skin on a fillet holds it in one piece and shields it from intense heat if the fire is too hot. If the skin is removed, you need to protect the fillet with aluminum foil cut to size. I recall cooking over an open fire on the shore on a fishing trip for peacock bass in Venezuela. The guides showed us how to prepare the bass and then how to wrap it correctly in aluminum foil for cooking. The results were delicious!

To cook on an open fire, you'll need a grate and picnic area fire rings (rocks) or anything else to contain the fire in a small area. Useful utensils include heavy-duty aluminum foil, flame-retardant gloves, a long-handled spatula and tongs, a grill basket, and a cast iron or heavy aluminum skillet for pan-frying.

The peacock bass I mentioned were cooked in aluminum foil over an open fire with the bass placed on a grate over the hot coals. You can wait until the wood burns down and you have only the hot coals and then lay the aluminum-foil-wrapped fish directly on the coals. Turn the aluminum foil every so often until the fish is done.

— OUTDOOR COOKING TIMES —

Outdoor cooking time varies considerably, depending upon the air temperature, wind, charcoal temperature, and distance of the fish from the coals. Here are some guidelines:

- For a whole fish weighing up to 2 pounds, cook at least 5 minutes on one side and 3 to 6 minutes on the second side.

- For fish weighing more than 2 to 3 pounds, cook 10 to 12 minutes per side.

- For fillets ¼ to ½ inch thick, cook 3 minutes on one side and 3 to 6 minutes on the second side.

- For fish wrapped in foil, add 1 to 2 minutes to the above times and check often.

— SMOKED FISH —

I've got an electric fish smoker and every once in a while I'll get a hankering for some smoked fish. Smoked fish is delicious and easy to prepare. Most anglers buy a smoker, though many enjoy making their own. Four items are needed to build a smoker: an enclosure to contain the heat and smoke, a source of heat (often an electric hot plate), wood chips or sawdust to provide smoke, and racks or bars to hold the fish. Many books are available with detailed instructions for building homemade smokers.

Smoke cooking (hot smoking) is the most popular method. It cooks the fish in a few hours, while adding a smoky flavor and a rich color. I use an electric Little Chief Smoker made by Luhr Jensen. I also own a big smoker that I use for smoking meats, which I can use for fish, too.

Here's my basic recipe for smoked fish (this recipe makes enough brine to soak 6 to 8 pounds of fish):

Fish or fish fillets

1 **cup salt**

10 **cups water**

¼ **cup granulated or packed brown sugar (optional)**

Bay leaf

Chili powder

Thyme

Put the fish or fillets in a non-metal container. In a separate bowl, mix together the remaining ingredients to make a brine solution. Pour the brine over the fish, and refrigerate. Soak up to 4 pounds of fish for 12 to 18 hours. For more than 4 pounds, soak for 24 to 48 hours. For fillets, fish steaks, or chunks ½ to 1 inch thick, soak 12 to 18 hours. Remove the fish and place it in the smoker for several hours, following the manufacturer's instructions.

— OVEN-COOKING FILLETS —

Fish can be broiled or baked in the oven. When cooking fillets with skin, place skin side up first. To broil, place most fish 4 inches from the heat. Place thin fillets 5 inches from the heat to keep them from drying. Line both the rack and pan of the broiler pan with aluminum foil for easy cleanup. Poke holes in the foil so the oil drains into the pan and you avoid flare-ups. If you're using an electric range, it is a good idea to leave the door slightly ajar. This keeps the heat constant since the broiling unit is always on. Close the door if using a gas range. Fish fillets usually take about 3 to 4 minutes to cook in a broiler, depending on thickness.

To bake fish fillets, place them in a baking pan that is large enough so they fit in a single layer without crowding. Place the pan on the center oven rack and bake at 350 degrees for about 10 to 12 minutes. If you wish, you can oven-fry your fish fillets. The advantage of oven-frying is that it makes the fish crisp, and browns the fish without much cooking oil. It also reduces frying odors. To oven-fry fish, simply cover the bottom of the pan with a thin layer of oil before baking.

— MICROWAVING —

Thawing fish in a microwave is easy if the fish are arranged so the least thawed parts are toward the outside of the plate. I separate frozen serving-size pieces before thawing. If this can't be done, break them apart as soon as possible.

Timing is critical when microwaving fish because it can be easily overcooked. Ideally, the fish should be removed from the oven just before it flakes. Watch carefully as it cooks. Basic microwaving calls for 100 percent power and about 2 to 5 minutes per pound.

⟶ FRYING FISH ⟵

My mother loved eating fish, and when my brother Jack brought home bluegill, catfish, crappie, and bass, Mother would batter them well and fry them in a big iron skillet. Years later, when I got married, my wife didn't know how to cook fish. So I recalled how my mother used to prepare her fish: she would wash the fish thoroughly, take her brown paper sack with cornmeal, salt, and pepper—maybe a little flour—then toss in the cleaned fish and shake the daylights out of that bag to coat the fish meat. Soon I was cooking delicious fish myself!

Over the years I picked up on new ideas on how to prepare fish. I've tried them all, but none can come close to the old method of cooking fish fillets or whole fish in cornmeal, salt, and pepper. I do not use an egg wash. I just toss my fish, a little bit damp from rinsing, in the cornmeal and other ingredients.

There are cooks that go all out in preparing their specialty mixes. I covered the Pickwick Catfish Cook-Off one year, and these cooks are super-serious about their mixes of flour and cornmeal. I tried every way I knew to get some of those mix recipes but had no luck. I was given a sack of the winning mix, and I tried to figure out what the ingredients were with no success.

Fishing has always been my favorite outdoor sport, so I wanted to master cooking fish. In talking with other cooks who prepared fish dishes, I learned the very first thing—and possibly the most important—about frying fish is the cooking oil. If the cooking oil isn't good quality, then nine out of ten times the fish you cook isn't going to be delicious.

Many of you have your own preference of oil. Mine is peanut oil. Any kind of oil will do if it will hold the right cooking temperature. Peanut oil doesn't break down and burn, and it can be used a number of times if strained and stored correctly.

Here are are few hints for preparing tasty fried fish:

- When batter-frying fish, make sure the batter is cold to prevent it from soaking up too much oil.

- Check to see if your oil is hot by dropping in a small piece of bread. It should brown within a minute.

- To keep earlier batches of fried fish crispy while cooking the rest, place cooked pieces in a warm oven on a wire rack over a paper-towel-lined plate.

⟶ A NOTE ON THE FISH RECIPES ⟵

I would like to emphasize again the importance of cleaning your catch. The cleaning will make or break a recipe. It's also important not to overcook fish. It becomes done sooner than most people realize.

We've got a lot of recipes for fish. Some recipes will say they're for bass or crappie, for instance, but you can interchange most fish. This means, for example, that you can swap sauger for crappie, bass, or catfish. However, trout can not necessarily be interchanged in recipes because it's an oily fish. I'm going to start with recipes in which you can use different kinds of fish.

— GENERAL FISH RECIPES FOR SPECIES — OF YOUR CHOICE

Creole Fish

Harold and Elizabeth Stiles
Chapmansboro, Tennessee

4	**fish fillets, about 4 ounces each**
1	**tablespoon lemon juice**
1	**cup Creole sauce (recipe follows)**

Preheat the oven to 350 degrees. Put the fillets in a lightly greased baking dish, and sprinkle with the lemon juice. Pour the Creole sauce over the fish. Cover, and bake in the oven for 25 minutes, or until the fish flakes easily.

MAKES 4 SERVINGS.

Creole Sauce

1	**tablespoon chopped onion**
3	**tablespoons chopped green pepper**
¼	**cup sliced mushrooms**
3	**tablespoons corn oil**
2	**cups stewed or fresh tomatoes**
1	**cup water**
½	**teaspoon salt**
	Dash of pepper
	Few drops of Tabasco (optional)
½	**teaspoon chopped basil (optional)**

Cook the onion, green pepper, and sliced mushrooms in the oil over low heat for 5 minutes. Add the tomatoes, water, and seasonings. Simmer until the sauce is thick, about 30 minutes.

MAKES 3 CUPS.

Broiler-Fried Fillets

⅓ cup buttermilk

⅛ teaspoon pepper

4   ounces crushed potato chips

¾ cup cornflake crumbs

¼ teaspoon paprika

1½ pounds fish fillets, at least ½ inch thick

Preheat the oven to 550 degrees or broil. Mix the buttermilk and pepper in a pie pan. Mix the crushed potato chips, cornflake crumbs, and paprika on a plate or waxed paper. Grease the broiler pan. Cut the fish into serving pieces and dip in the buttermilk mixture. Coat with the potato chip mixture, and place on the broiler pan. Broil 6 inches from the heat for 3 minutes per side, or until the fish flakes easily.

MAKES 6 SERVINGS.

Basic Fried Fish

1 to 2 pounds fish fillets

Salt and pepper

1   beaten egg

½ cup all-purpose flour or cornmeal

Vegetable oil for frying

Cut the fillets into desired serving sizes. Salt and pepper to taste. Dip the fillets in egg, and then roll in flour or cornmeal. Fry the fillets in approximately ⅓ inch of vegetable oil in a medium-size skillet. Fry for 4 to 5 minutes per side. Remove the fish, and place on paper towels to drain.

MAKES 6 TO 8 SERVINGS.

Many lakes become muddy after heavy rains, and the lower areas of the lakes are usually not as muddy as the upper sections. Feeder creeks will clear before the main lake does.

The Famous Beer Batter

Anonymous

2   cups all-purpose flour

1   egg

1   tablespoon garlic salt

1   teaspoon salt

1   tablespoon lemon pepper

1   can of your favorite beer

1   cup cornflake crumbs or cornmeal

10 to 12 fish fillets

Mix the flour, egg, garlic, salt, and lemon pepper in a large bowl. Add the beer until the batter is thin but not watery. Dip the dry fish in the batter, and roll in the cornflakes or cornmeal. Fry the fish in a medium-size skillet until golden brown. Use a small amount of vegetable oil in the skillet to prevent sticking.

MAKES 10 TO 12 SERVINGS.

Tabasco Fish

I heard about this recipe at a wild game dinner. I thought it had to be hotter than a two-dollar pistol, but I was told that it wasn't hot at all because the "heat" is removed when it is deep-fried. So I tried the recipe, and let me tell you, these folks knew what they were talking about. It was terrific. Not hot at all, yet the Tabasco flavoring added a wonderfully different taste to the fried fish.   —JIMMY

Fish fillets

Tabasco

All-purpose flour

Cornmeal

Salt

Oil for frying

Put the fish fillets in a bowl or deep dish. Sprinkle the fish with Tabasco. Toss the fish around in the Tabasco really well, and then lay them in your flour-cornmeal mix. The mix should not be peppered, just salted the way you usually prepare a mix. Place the fish gently into a skillet or wire basket, and deep-fry them until they float and are golden brown.

Mustard Fried Fish

12   panfish
      or
6   larger fish fillets

1   (16-ounce) carton sour cream

1   cup prepared mustard

3   cups yellow cornmeal

    Salt and pepper

    Peanut oil for frying

Coat the fish with the sour cream and mustard, and let stand for 20 minutes in the refrigerator. Season the cornmeal with salt and pepper to taste before dredging the fish in the mixture. Deep-fry the fish in hot peanut oil, using either a cast iron skillet or deep fryer.

MAKES 4 TO 6 SERVINGS.

You can make a crankbait run deeper by adding a worm weight or split shot to the line just ahead of the lure.

Lemon Rind Fried Fish

Barry Masson
Knoxville, Tennessee

1½ cups flour

2   teaspoons grated lemon peel

½   teaspoon salt

¼   teaspoon pepper

1   cup beer or water

    Vegetable oil for frying

1½ pounds fish fillets or panfish

½   cup cornmeal for coating

Mix together 1 cup of the flour, the lemon peel, salt, pepper, and beer. Chill for 30 minutes. Heat 2 inches of the oil in a fryer to 375 degrees. Mix the cornmeal and the remaining ½ cup flour for coating. Coat the fish in the cornmeal-flour mixture. Dip in the batter. Fry 3 minutes or until tender.

MAKES 2 TO 4 SERVINGS.

Herbed and Fried Fish

1   pound fish fillets or
    panfish

¼   cup all-purpose flour

1   egg

½   tablespoon milk

1   (1-pound) box saltine
    crackers, crushed

½   teaspoon parsley flakes

½   teaspoon sweet basil

¼   teaspoon oregano

⅛   teaspoon garlic powder

½   cup grated Parmesan cheese

½   cup butter-flavored
    shortening

Pat the fish fillets dry with paper towels. Dredge the fish in the flour and shake off the excess. Mix the egg and milk in a bowl. In a separate bowl, mix the crackers, parsley, basil, oregano, garlic powder, and Parmesan cheese. Dip the fish in the egg mixture, then in the cracker mix. In a frying pan, heat the shortening to 425 to 450 degrees. Place the breaded fish in the pan, skin side up. Fry until golden brown.

MAKES 4 SERVINGS.

Cajun Fillets

½   cup all-purpose flour or
    pancake mix

¼   cup milk

1   egg

1   cup cornmeal

1   tablespoon Cajun
    seasoning

½   teaspoon salt

¼   teaspoon pepper

1   pound fish fillets
    Oil for frying

Mix the flour, milk, and egg in a small bowl. Mix the cornmeal, Cajun seasoning, salt, and pepper in another small bowl. Dip the fillets in the wet mixture to completely moisten the surface; then roll in the dry mixture. Fry the fillets in the oil in a medium-size skillet until both sides are golden brown. Serve with pepper or Tabasco.

MAKES 4 SERVINGS.

Canadian Battered Fish Sandwiches

Larry Bell
Chattanooga, Tennessee

I work with a fellow who is lucky enough to fish in Canada every year. He always returns from his annual trip talking about the fish he caught and the great shore lunches prepared by the fishing guide. He brought back this recipe for the fish batter used in those famous shore lunches.
—LARRY BELL

2   cups pancake flour
1   cup cornflake crumbs
¼   cup yellow cornmeal
1   tablespoon garlic salt
6   fish fillets
2   beaten eggs
    Oil for frying
    Sandwich buns
1   jar Cheez Whiz (optional)

Place the flour, crumbs, cornmeal, and garlic salt in a large Ziploc bag, and shake to ensure that all the ingredients are well mixed. Dip the fish fillets in the beaten eggs, and place the fillets in the dry mixture. Give the bag a few shakes to coat the fillets, and deep-fry in hot vegetable oil. Serve the golden brown fillets on the sandwich buns. Add Cheez Whiz to the sandwich if desired.

MAKES 3 TO 6 SERVINGS.

Fish and Kraut Sandwiches

Barry Masson
Knoxville, Tennessee

1   cup cooked, flaked fish
½   cup well-drained sauerkraut
¼   cup chopped dill pickles
¼   cup mayonnaise
1   tablespoon horseradish
12 slices rye bread
4   (1-ounce) slices Swiss cheese
2   tablespoons margarine

In a mixing bowl, combine the fish, sauerkraut, pickles, mayonnaise, and horseradish. Mix well. Spread the mixture evenly on half the bread slices. Top with the cheese slices. Top with the remaining bread slices. Melt the margarine in a skillet. Place the sandwiches in the skillet, and grill on each side until golden brown.

MAKES 4 SERVINGS.

Launching ramps are busy places. And some folks don't know how to launch or retrieve their boats as fast as we wish they could. Remember how somebody showed you how to launch and retrieve your boat quickly? Now you can return the favor. Stand close to the ramp, and when you see an opportunity to assist a fellow boater, offer to help. Now, instead of wishing he would hurry up, you can show him a faster way.

Tennessee Paella

Iris B. Coffey
Lobelville, Tennessee

1   (12 ounce) container white fillets, defrosted if frozen

1   tablespoon sherry

1¼ cups cooked white rice

½   tablespoon pimientos

3   tablespoons finely chopped green onions

3   tablespoons chopped mushrooms, fresh or canned

3   tablespoons chopped turkey ham or luncheon ham

3   tablespoons finely chopped green peppers

   Salt and pepper

1   tablespoon olive oil or canola oil

½   tablespoon pimientos, for topping

4   cherry tomatoes, halved

½   cup grated yellow cheese

Preheat the oven to 325 degrees. Marinate the defrosted fish pieces in sherry for no more than 5 minutes. While marinating the fish, combine the rice, pimientos, onions, mushrooms, ham, green peppers, salt and pepper to taste, and oil. Press into a greased 9-inch pie pan, and place the fish on top. Place the pimiento and halved cherry tomatoes between the fish pieces. It should look like a pizza pie. Scatter the cheese over the fish, and cover with foil. Cook in the oven for 20 to 25 minutes.

MAKES 4 SERVINGS.

Cream Cheese Fish Bake

Barry Masson
Knoxville, Tennessee

1   (3-ounce) package cream cheese
1   cup uncooked macaroni
1   (10 ¾-ounce) can condensed cream of mushroom soup
1½ cups cooked, flaked fish
¼   cup chopped onion
¼   cup chopped green pepper
2   tablespoons prepared mustard
¼   teaspoon salt
¼   cup milk
½   cup cornflake crumbs

Preheat the oven to 375 degrees. Allow the cream cheese to soften at room temperature. Prepare the macaroni according to package directions. Drain. Blend the soup and cream cheese with an electric mixer. Stir in the macaroni, fish, onion, green pepper, mustard, salt, and milk. Place the mixture in a 1½-quart dish. Sprinkle with the cornflake crumbs. Bake for 20 to 25 minutes.

MAKES 4 SERVINGS.

Fish Cakes

Gerry Szalay
Nashville, Tennessee

This is delicious—just try it. We ate this in Newfoundland, where it is one of the favorite native dishes. However, I could not get the recipe, so I had to experiment with one.
— GERRY SZALAY

1   cup leftover cooked fish, crumbled, or put a few pieces in the microwave to cook
½   cup mashed potatoes
½   cup chopped onion
    Garlic salt
    Blackened seasoning
    Cornmeal
    Oil for frying

Mix the fish, potatoes, and onion with garlic salt and blackened seasoning to taste. Shape into patties, roll in the cornmeal, and fry.

MAKES 2 TO 3 SERVINGS.

Smoked Fish Dip

1 cup sour cream

½ cup mayonnaise or salad dressing

1 cup flaked smoked fish

3 tablespoons chopped green onion

½ teaspoon Worcestershire sauce

Dash garlic powder

In a small bowl blend the sour cream and mayonnaise. Stir in the fish, onion, Worcestershire sauce, and garlic. Cover and refrigerate at least 1 hour. Serve as a dip for chips or vegetables.

MAKES ABOUT ½ CUP.

— CATFISH —

Grilled Barbecued Catfish

Mrs. James R. Miller

6 small to medium catfish

1 teaspoon Worcestershire sauce

¼ teaspoon paprika

½ cup salad oil

¼ cup white vinegar

¼ cup catsup

2 tablespoons sugar

¼ teaspoon salt

¼ teaspoon pepper

Clean and fillet the catfish. Combine the Worcestershire sauce, paprika, salad oil, vinegar, catsup, sugar, salt, and pepper. Place the fish in the mixture for 30 minutes before grilling. Cook 3 to 4 inches from the hot coals on a well-greased grill for about 5 minutes per side, or until the fish tests done. Brush often with the sauce while barbecuing. Catfish should be skinned for best results.

MAKES 6 SERVINGS.

THE CATFISH SISTERS

Mrs. Madge Thomas, who lives near Bellevue, Tennessee, tells this story about fishing with her sister, Mrs. Julia Kelley, who lives near Ashland City. These sisters are now in their seventies and have been fishing together for more than 50 years. From this story, it sounds like they both know their fishing.

They were fishing from the bank with Daiwa bait-casting reels with 17-pound test line. Mrs. Thomas says her sister "plugs all the time for bass." They were on the east bank of Kentucky Lake near Hurstburg, where they have "caught some good bass," as Mrs. Thomas put it.

"We catch a lot of bass in the river. We go through Big Bottoms and fish where the pipes empty into the river, where there's a lot of current. It's a real good place to fish, and we've caught all kinds down there, but we've never experienced anything like this."

Bass fishing was dead that day so they switched to small crappie jigs with a small curly tail. "She (Mrs. Kelley) was just fishing with it and all of a sudden she thought she was hung," says Mrs. Thomas. "She caught this big catfish. I mean it was the biggest thing you have ever seen. We had to have help to get it out. We couldn't lift it by ourselves. It weighed 50 pounds."

She says the little crappie jig was embedded in the corner of the fish's mouth. "It took over 30 minutes to land it. It's a good thing she had 17-pound test line. She could get it to the bank but couldn't see what it was. When it came close to the bank, it would take off. She couldn't do anything with it, and it ran right back out into the boiling water that was coming out of those pipes."

Fortunately, a young man came by to help them. "I was running to the car that was about a block away to get a gaff my sister bought when she was fishing down in Florida. But there was no way that she and I could have lifted that fish up the bank. I've forgotten the young man's name, but he said everyone knew him as 'Corn Bread.' He got down and pulled the fish up the bank for us."

Corn Bread told the ladies his father had fished trotlines there for 40 years and hadn't caught a cat that large. Another person told them it was a record fish for that area. Twenty-eight pounds was the largest catfish anyone had heard of from around there.

"We kind of hated to take him, because he looked so old. But my sister wanted to mount the head. The head was 12 inches across and the fish was 48 inches long. My sister gave the fish to her daughter, and she said it was the prettiest white meat. I've forgotten how much she said it weighed after cleaning, but it was a lot of fish."

Mrs. Thomas says that one lady fishing close to them made it even more fun. "I wish I had had my video camera to tape her. She just went wild when she saw that fish. She was so excited she was jumping around. It was comical."

Mrs. Thomas says her sister's comment about the fish was, "Why couldn't it have been a bass?"

Herb-Baked Catfish

1   **pound catfish**

1   **tablespoon butter**

1   **cup milk**

2   **tablespoons all-purpose flour**

$\frac{1}{4}$ **teaspoon salt**

$\frac{1}{4}$ **teaspoon garlic salt**

$\frac{1}{8}$ **teaspoon pepper**

$\frac{1}{8}$ **teaspoon dried thyme**

 Dash of oregano

$\frac{1}{4}$ **cup sliced green onions**

 Paprika

Place the fish in a baking dish. Dot with the butter. Thoroughly blend the milk and flour in a pan. Cook over medium heat, stirring until the sauce thickens and bubbles. Cook and stir 1 minute longer. Stir in the salt, garlic salt, pepper, thyme, oregano, and green onion. Preheat the oven to 350 degrees. Pour the sauce over the fish. Sprinkle with paprika. Bake in the oven, uncovered, for 20 to 25 minutes.

MAKES 4 SERVINGS.

Deep-Fried Catfish

Mrs. Gary Lee Pollitt
Cookeville , Tennessee

Oil for frying
¼ cup yellow cornmeal
¼ cup flour
Salt and pepper
6 skinned catfish (heads and tails removed)
1 egg, beaten

Heat the oil in a saucepan to 425 degrees. In a medium bowl, mix the cormeal, flour, and salt and pepper to taste. Dip the fish in the mixture; then dip the fish in the egg and again in the meal-flour mixture. Fry 3 to 6 minutes, depending on the size of the fish.

MAKES 6 TO 12 SERVINGS.

Southern Fried Catfish

Bill Flenn

Vegetable oil for frying
¼ cup prepared mustard
½ teaspoon paprika
½ cup all-purpose flour
2 cups yellow cornmeal
Salt and pepper
Cayenne
2 cups buttermilk
¼ cup Tabasco
12 catfish fillets, halved

Heat the oil in a large skillet or deep fat fryer. Combine the mustard, paprika, flour, cornmeal, salt, pepper, and cayenne to taste in a medium mixing bowl. Add the buttermilk and Tabasco, and mix well. Dip the fish in the buttermilk mixture, dust with the flour, dip again in the mixture, and roll in the cornmeal. Drop the fish into the hot oil, and cook 6 to 8 minutes, or until brown. Drain well on paper towels.

MAKES 12 SERVINGS.

Cajun Spicy Fried Catfish

James Naquin
Murfreesboro, Tennessee

My family is from a little town about 60 miles south of New Orleans called Houma—better known as Sportsman's Paradise. Here's a Cajun recipe you'll enjoy.

—JAMES NAQUIN

1 envelope Shake & Bake for pork

3 tablespoons sifted flour

1 cup instant potato flakes

4 tablespoons cornmeal

Salt and pepper

2–3 pounds sliced fish

½ cup buttermilk

Hot sauce

Oil for frying

Mix the Shake & Bake, flour, potato flakes, and cornmeal. Salt and pepper the fish to taste. Mix the buttermilk and hot sauce, and pour over the fish. Toss to coat evenly. Press the dry mixture on each piece of fish, coating well. Pan-fry until brown. Turn with a spatula to prevent breaking. The potatoes seal the fish and keep it moist.

MAKES 4 TO 6 SERVINGS.

I hate to fish when it's windy, but you shouldn't avoid the wind when you are fishing. Wind can blow insects and plankton into shore and attract minnows, which in turn attract bass. It also stirs up the water and makes it easier for bass to ambush their prey. Keep the wind at your back, and it can actually help you cast farther as you probe breeze-swept shorelines.

Blackened Catfish

Gary Gillispie
Nashville, Tennessee

Don't forget the cold beer with this spicy recipe. —GARY GILLISPIE

2 teaspoons paprika

2½ teaspoons salt

1 teaspoon onion powder

1½ teaspoons garlic

1½ teaspoons cayenne

2 teaspoons lemon pepper marinade

1 teaspoon ground thyme

1½ teaspoons basil

6 catfish fillets

8 ounces (1 stick) unsalted butter, melted

Lemon wedges

Heat Mama's old iron skillet over high heat until a drop of water sizzles in the pan, or about 10 minutes. Combine the paprika, salt, onion powder, garlic, cayenne, lemon pepper marinade, thyme, and basil, and anything else you can get your hands on, in a good-size bowl. Keep fillets cold next to the beer until ready to use. Dip each fillet in the melted butter so that its sides are slippery. Sprinkle the seasoning mix on both sides, and place them on waxed paper while preparing other fillets. Place 3 fillets in your skillet (I hope it's the one you heated), and drizzle each piece of fish with 1 tablespoon of melted butter. (You will think Grandpa is there with his cigar burning trash because there will be a lot of smoke. Make sure you are in a well-ventilated place.) Cook quickly, about 2 minutes per side. Remove and repeat the process until all fillets are cooked. Serve immediately with the lemon wedges.

MAKES 6 SERVINGS.

Fish face upstream in current. A natural presentation is to cast upstream and retrieve your lure downstream so the fish can see it coming.

Catfish Stew

5 **pounds catfish**

½ **pound bacon, diced**

3 **pounds red potatoes, diced**

2 **pounds white onions, diced**

5 **cups water**

6 **hard-cooked eggs, diced**

1 **(4-ounce) can pimiento, drained and diced**

1 **(6-ounce) can evaporated milk**

Salt and pepper

Fry the fish (use a recipe with cornmeal, milk, and seasonings) until the flesh flakes when poked with a fork. Fry the bacon until crisp and remove from the skillet. Fry the potatoes and onion in the bacon drippings until tender. Place the fish in 4 cups of the water in a cast iron Dutch oven. Add the bacon, potatoes, onion, eggs, and pimiento. Simmer for 1 to 1½ hours, adding more water if needed. Add the milk, stirring constantly, while seasoning with the salt and pepper to taste.

MAKES 10 TO 15 SERVINGS.

— CRAPPIE —

Foiled Crappie

2 **pounds crappie fillets**

3 **tablespoons butter**

3 **teaspoons lemon juice**

½ **teaspoon basil**

½ **teaspoon dill**

Salt and pepper

Rub the fillets with the butter, and place on aluminum foil. Sprinkle the lemon juice, basil, dill, salt, and pepper on the fillets. Fold the foil over the fillets, and tightly seal edges. Grill or bake for approximately 15 minutes, or until the fillets are white and flaky.

MAKES 6 TO 8 SERVINGS.

Grilled Parmesan Crappie

Fresh crappie fillets

Lemon juice

Butter or margarine

Seasoned salt

Fresh grated Parmesan cheese

Diced green peppers

Diced onions

Fold a sheet of aluminum foil in two and form into a small "dish." Pour enough lemon juice in the foil to cover the bottom, and put the fillets in the juice. Place a generous amount of butter on top of each fillet, and sprinkle each with seasoned salt and Parmesan cheese. Add the diced green peppers and onions, and use another piece of foil to completely enclose the fillets by folding over all edges. Grill for 5 to 6 minutes on each side. Drain juices and serve.

MAKES 6 SERVINGS.

Crappie have a thin membrane around their mouths that will tear wth a hard hook-set. Your chances of landing the fish are better if you lift your rod firmly rather than jerking it.

Baked Parmesan Crappie

Iris B. Coffey
Lobelville, Tennessee

¼ cup Parmesan cheese

¼ cup seasoned bread crumbs

1 tablespoon melted butter or margarine

4 tablespoons fresh parsley

1–2 pounds crappie fillets

Preheat the oven to 325 degrees. Mix the Parmesan cheese, bread crumbs, butter, and parsley in a small bowl. Sprinkle the mixture on the fillets placed in a greased baking pan. Bake in the oven for 15 to 20 minutes.

MAKES 4 TO 8 SERVINGS.

Crusty Crappie

Mayme Walker
McMinnville, Tennessee

¼ **cup white or wine vinegar**

1 **pound crappie fillets (or bass, walleye, etc.)**

¼ **cup cornmeal**

½ **teaspoon paprika**

Salt and pepper

2 **tablespoons melted diet margarine**

Preheat oven to 450 degrees. Pour the vinegar into a shallow dish, and dip the fillets on each side to moisten. Combine the cornmeal and paprika in a shallow dish, and coat the fillets on both sides with the mixture. Salt and pepper to taste, and sprinkle any remaining cornmeal over fillets. Place the fish on a nonstick baking sheet or foil sprayed with nonstick cooking spray. Drizzle the margarine evenly over the fillets. Bake 20 to 25 minutes or until golden brown.

MAKES 4 SERVINGS.

Oven-Fried Crappie

1 **pound crappie fillets**

⅓ **cup cornmeal**

⅓ **cup bread crumbs**

½ **teaspoon paprika**

¼ **teaspoon dill weed**

Salt and pepper

⅓ **cup milk**

3 **tablespoons butter or margarine**

Preheat the oven to 425 degrees. Cut the fillets into desired serving sizes. Combine the cornmeal, bread crumbs, paprika, and dill weed in a medium-size bowl. Add salt and pepper to taste. Pour the milk into a small bowl. Dip the fish in the milk, and roll in the dry mixture. Place the fillets on a cookie sheet or baking pan, and drizzle butter over each fillet. Bake in the oven for about 12 minutes, or until the fillets are moist and flaky.

MAKES 4 SERVINGS.

Simple Oven-Fried Crappie

Vegetable, canola, or
peanut oil

1 egg

¼ cup milk

1 pound crappie fillets

1 cup Italian-style bread
crumbs

Salt and pepper

Preheat the oven to 425 degrees. Pour the oil into a medium-size casserole dish to a depth of approximately ⅛ inch, and heat in the oven. Combine the egg and milk in a small bowl, and beat until completely mixed. Dip the fillets in the milk-egg mixture, and then roll in the bread crumbs. Add salt and pepper to taste. Place the fillets in the heated pan of oil, allow the oil to soak into the first side, and then turn the fillets over to oil the second side. Bake 8 to 10 minutes, or until golden brown.

MAKES 4 SERVINGS.

Nuked Crappie

Barry Masson
Knoxville, Tennessee

Fresh crappie fillets

Butter or margarine

Lemon pepper

Other spices (optional)

Rub the fillets with butter, completely covering each fillet. Sprinkle with lemon pepper (and/or any other spice to your liking). Cover fillets with a paper towel or plastic wrap to retain moisture. Microwave until the fillets become white and flaky. Let cool to serving temperature and enjoy.

SERVINGS WILL DEPEND ON THE AMOUNT OF FISH PREPARED.

Nuked Buttermilk Crappie

Barry Masson
Knoxville, Tennessee

Fresh crappie fillets

Buttermilk

Lemon juice

Salt and pepper

Soak the fillets in the buttermilk, and sprinkle them with the lemon juice and salt and pepper to taste. Wrap the fillets in a paper towel to hold in the moisture and avoid drying out. Microwave for 3 to 4 minutes, or until white and flaky.

SERVINGS WILL DEPEND ON THE AMOUNT OF FISH PREPARED.

Beer-Battered Fried Crappie

This is one of the most popular recipes for frying fish. —JIMMY

1 **cup flour**

1 **teaspoon baking soda**

1 **teaspoon baking powder**

1 **cup flat beer**

2 **eggs**

8 **crappie fillets**

Mix the flour, baking soda, baking powder, and beer. Beat the eggs lightly and add to the mixture. Beat the entire mixture until creamy. Dip the dry fillets in the batter, and deep-fry at 375 degrees until golden brown.

MAKES 4 SERVINGS.

Fast Fried Crappie

1/3 **pound crappie fillets per person**

Salt

Lemon pepper

2 **cups dry pancake mix**

Oil for frying

Cocktail sauce

Wash the fish, and then dip into fresh water. Sprinkle with the salt and lemon pepper. Coat lightly with the pancake mix. Fry in deep fat for 4 or 5 minutes, or until the fish flakes easily. Serve with the cocktail sauce.

MAKES 6 SERVINGS WHEN USING 2 POUNDS FISH.

GEORGE GREGORY: JIGS AND ROSES

George Gregory of Lynchburg is probably the best known crappie angler in Moore County, as well as the town's most respected horticulturist. George has developed a green thumb working at the Jack Daniel's Distillery for the last 20-something years. His specialty is roses—when he's not fishing his homemade jigs on Normandy or Tims Ford.

When asked how he got started making jigs, he said, "I saw pouring jigs demonstrated on *Tennessee Outdoorsmen.* I had always made my jigs with spilt shot on a hook, but after seeing that, I got molds and lead and poured my own. I make them just like I want, designs you can't find in a bait shop.

"I can make them to look just like a minnow or the opposite of a minnow. I think they'll hit those funny-colored jigs because they are curious about them, not because they are hungry. I make lots of $\frac{1}{32}$-ounce jigs for crappie.

"I'll use yellow or orange on a red head jig in stained water. If the water is clear, I'll use yellow and chartreuse. I use the brighter colors when the water is dingy.

"In October I use 4-pound test line because the water has some color, the fish aren't going to be as deep, and I'm going to be catching bigger fish. In summer, with the clear water, I have to use 2-pound test. Four-pound test line lets the jig work well, and the larger diameter line lets it fall a little slower, keeping the bait in the strike zone longer. The 4-pound test holds better in rough cover, but some of those big crappie will still break it.

"I used to use $\frac{1}{16}$-ounce jigs, but they fall too fast. They'll drop past suspended fish too fast; that's why I only use $\frac{1}{32}$-ounce now.

"You have to use a 6- or $6\frac{1}{2}$-foot spinning rod with a slow tip to cast these jigs effectively. I cast out 20 to 30 feet, let my jig sink, and slowly reel it in, always watching my line. I fish shallow or deep the same way. I just start reeling sooner when fishing shallow."

George was a featured guest on a *Tennessee Outdoorsmen* program. He was chauffeured by limousine from the Jack Daniel's Distillery in Lynchburg for the broadcast featuring him catching crappie on Normandy Lake. These are recipes that he and his wife, Louise, developed.

THE GREGORYS' SPECIAL FRIED CRAPPIE

Vegetable oil or
shortening for frying

2 cups self-rising
cornmeal

2 tablespoons all-
purpose flour

Black pepper

4 eggs, beaten

3 pounds crappie fillets

Heat the oil in a large skillet or in a fryer to 360 degrees. Combine the cornmeal, flour, and pepper in a shallow bowl. Beat the eggs in another bowl. Dry the fillets with a paper towel. Dredge the fillets in the eggs, then in the cornmeal mixture, back in the eggs, and then again in the cornmeal. Let the coated fillets sit a few minutes before cooking. Fry until golden brown.

MAKES 6 TO 8 SERVINGS.

Variation:

To make Fried Crappie Fingers, simply cut the fillets into bite-size pieces and serve with the following dipping sauce.

Louise's Special Jack Daniel's Red Cocktail Dipping Sauce

1½ cups catsup

2 tablespoons brown
sugar

2 tablespoons
Worcestershire sauce

1 tablespoon dry
mustard

⅓ cup Jack Daniel's
Tennessee Whiskey

Combine the catsup, brown sugar, Worcestershire sauce, and dry mustard in a small saucepan. Bring to a boil, stirring occasionally. Stir in the whiskey and simmer 5 minutes. Refrigerate until serving time.

MAKES ABOUT 2 CUPS SAUCE FOR DIPPING CRAPPIE FINGERS.

Potato Crappie Fillets

I don't like instant potatoes as a rule, but they make this recipe work. My recipe says blackened seasoning is optional, but don't believe it. —VERN

⅓ cup all-purpose flour

Salt and pepper

Blackened seasoning (optional)

2 eggs

1 cup instant potato flakes

1 pound crappie fillets

Vegetable oil for frying

Combine the flour, salt and pepper to taste, and the blackened seasoning, if using, in a medium-size bowl, and mix. Beat the eggs in a small bowl until smooth. Pour the potato flakes onto a large plate or wax paper on the countertop. Roll the fillets in the seasoning mixture, dip in the eggs to wet, and then roll in the potato flakes. Fry in the oil in a heavy, medium-size skillet until golden brown.

MAKES 4 SERVINGS.

— TROUT —

Grilled Trout

James Naquin
Murfreesboro, Tennessee

6–8 whole trout

¼ pound (1 stick) butter or margarine

1 cup chopped green onion

Salt and pepper

Garlic powder

2 tablespoons dehydrated parsley flakes

Inside the trout cavities place 1 tablespoon of the butter, chopped onion, and salt, pepper, and garlic powder to taste. Sprinkle the outside with parsley flakes and a little salt and pepper. Double wrap the trout, one to a package, in aluminum foil. Place on the grill, cook 7 to 10 minutes on one side, turn, and cook 5 minutes more.

MAKES 4 TO 6 SERVINGS.

Lure speed, in some cases, is the forgotten variable when it comes to catching fish on crankbaits. Most crankbaits will achieve their maximum diving depth at speeds ranging from 1 to 3 mph. But at what speed do the fish want the lure? That's another consideration, and the only way to discover the answer is by constantly experimenting until the fish tell you by striking.

Broiled Trout with Topping

2 **tablespoons melted butter**	Preheat the oven to broil. Melt the butter in a shallow pan, add the trout fillets, and broil until they flake, turning once. While this is cooking, prepare the topping. When the fillets are done, spoon the topping over them. Sprinkle generously with Parmesan cheese. Serve immediately.
2 **pounds trout fillets**	
Topping (recipe follows)	
Parmesan cheese	

MAKES 2 TO 4 SERVINGS.

Topping

½ **cup sliced fresh mushrooms**	Sauté the mushrooms and onions in the butter until slightly tender.
¼ **cup chopped fresh green onions (include tops)**	
1 **teaspoon butter**	

Trout Kabobs

Dee Kirkpatrick
Nashville, Tennessee

1   large green pepper

1   quart water

4   small onions (about ½ pound)

2   pounds trout or other oily fish fillets or steaks, skin removed

16 French bread cubes, 1½ x 1½ inches thick

4   metal skewers, 15 inches long

1   cup margarine or butter

¼   teaspoon garlic salt

4   lemon wedges

Set the oven to broil or 550 degrees. Core and seed the pepper, and cut in half. In a 3-quart saucepan, heat the water to boiling. Add the green peppers and onions, and cover. Cook over high heat for 4 minutes. Drain. Rinse under cold, running water, and drain. Cut the onions in half, and cut the green pepper into 1-inch pieces. Cut the fish into 1-inch chunks. Alternately thread 2 onion halves, ¼ of the green pepper pieces, ¼ of the fish, and 4 bread cubes on each skewer. Place the kabobs on a lightly greased broiler pan. In a 1-quart saucepan, heat the margarine and garlic salt over medium heat until the margarine is melted. Brush the margarine on the fish, bread, and vegetables. Broil the kabobs 8 to 9 inches from the heat, turning and brushing with margarine 4 times until the fish flakes easily at the thickest part, about 8 minutes. Serve the kabobs with the lemon wedges.

MAKES 4 TO 6 SERVINGS.

Give your spinnerbaits a different look by painting one side of each blade. There's no end to the visual effects you can create by experimenting with various flat, bright, or reflective colors.

Baked Trout

Dee Kirkpatrick
Nashville, Tennessee

Fresh lemon juice

4 trout, with or without heads
(or bass or salmon)

Salt and pepper

Lemon slices

Butter

Onion slices (optional)

Parsley flakes

Fresh parsley

Preheat the oven to 325 degrees. Sprinkle the lemon juice over thoroughly cleaned fish. Salt and pepper the fish to taste, and place the lemon slices and pats of the butter on the fish. Raw onion slices may be used, too. Sprinkle the fish with parsley flakes. Bake 1- to 1½ -pound fish for 30 to 40 minutes; fish 2½ pounds or heavier take 1 to 1¼ hours. Serve with additional lemon slices and fresh parsley.

MAKES 2 TO 4 SERVINGS.

Foil-Baked Trout

2½ pounds trout fillets

3 teaspoons lemon juice

3 tablespoons melted butter

Salt and pepper

Parsley

Basil

Dill

Heat the grill or preheat the oven to 350 degrees. Place the fish on aluminum foil sprayed with cooking spray. Drizzle the lemon juice and butter over the fish. Salt and pepper the fish to taste, and add parsley, basil, and dill. Fold the edges of the foil to form a tight seal. Grill for 15 minutes on high until the meat is flaky, or cook in the oven.

MAKES 2 TO 4 SERVINGS.

Sassy Rainbow Trout

Cathy Summerlin
Leipers Fork, Tennessee

4	rainbow trout fillets
	Salt and pepper
4	tablespoons olive oil
2	egg yolks
2	sticks butter or margarine
1	tablespoon lemon juice
1	cup cooked chopped shrimp
½	cup crabmeat
½	cup sliced mushrooms
2	tablespoons dry white wine
2 to 4	drops Tabasco

Preheat the oven to 375 degrees. Dry the fillets, and season with salt and pepper to taste. Place in a baking dish, add the oil, and bake in the oven for about 20 minutes. Make the sauce while the fish bake. Put the 2 egg yolks in the top of a double boiler over hot, but not boiling, water, and beat until slightly thickened. Melt the butter, and slowly add it to the egg yolks, stirring constantly until the mixture thickens. Add the lemon juice, shrimp, crabmeat, mushrooms, wine, and Tabasco. Mix well, and season to taste with salt and pepper. Stir and cook for 10 minutes longer. Raise the oven temperature to broil. Place the baked fillets on an ovenproof platter. Spoon the sauce over the fish, and place it under the broiler, browning slightly.

MAKES 2 TO 4 SERVINGS.

Baked Trout with Tomato and Onion

1	pound trout
1	tablespoon chopped parsley
1	tablespoon lemon juice
¾	teaspoon salt
3	tablespoons olive oil
1	medium onion, thinly sliced
1	clove garlic, minced
1	large tomato, thinly sliced
1	lemon, thinly sliced
2	tablespoons white wine (or water)

Preheat the oven to 350 degrees. Arrange the fish in an 8- or 9-inch-square baking dish. Sprinkle with the parsley, lemon juice, and salt. Heat the oil in a skillet, and sauté the onion and garlic until limp. Top the fish with the onion mixture and oil from skillet. Arrange the tomato slices on top of the onion mixture, and place the lemon slices on top. Pour wine or water over all, and bake in the oven for 30 to 35 minutes, or until fish flakes easily.

MAKES 4 SERVINGS.

Terminal tackle for bait fishing is very important. Don't use more than you need. Allow at least 8 to 16 inches of line between the bait and the sinkers so that the bait drifts in the current naturally. Choose a "sensitive" float that will barely stay on the surface. It is more responsive to a bite.

Baked Trout in Sour Cream

3 to 4 medium trout fillets

    Butter or margarine

    Salt and pepper

1 (6-ounce) container sour cream

Preheat the oven to 350 degrees. Arrange the fish in a shallow baking dish. Dot with butter or margarine. Sprinkle with salt and pepper to taste. Cover with a liberal amount of the sour cream. Bake in the oven for 50 to 60 minutes or until done. Serve with rice.

MAKES 2 TO 4 SERVINGS.

Wined Rainbow Trout

Ellen Bilodeau
Scottsville, Kentucky

4 rainbow trout

    Salt and pepper

2 cups all-purpose flour

2 tablespoons butter

1 tablespoon olive oil

3 tablespoons lemon juice

½ cup dry white wine

Sprinkle the trout inside and out with salt and pepper. Place the flour in a large resealable bag, and add one fish at a time, shaking to thoroughly coat. In a large cast iron skillet, heat the butter and oil over medium-high heat. Add the trout, and sauté on each side for 2 minutes or until the skin is golden brown. Add the lemon juice, and simmer for 2 minutes. Add the wine, cover, and simmer another 3 minutes, or until the trout flesh is opaque. Pour the skillet juices over the trout and serve.

MAKES 2 TO 4 SERVINGS.

Smoked Marinated Trout

John "Bubba" Woodfin
Murfreesboro, Tennessee

1	stick butter
1	cup honey
3	teaspoons lemon pepper
1	teaspoon blackened seasoning
6	trout fillets

Mix the butter, honey, lemon pepper, and blackened seasoning. Cut grooves into the fillet, and then brush the fillet well with the marinade, filling the grooves. Put the trout into a stove-top smoker set at medium. Use hickory sawdust in the bottom of the smoker. Put the fillet on a rack, cover with a lid, and cook for 15 to 20 minutes. Slide the lid open, and marinate the meat again. Close the lid and cook for another 5 to 10 minutes.

MAKES 6 SERVINGS.
Note: You may use an outdoor smoker.

— TRUE BASS (STRIPERS, HYBRIDS, AND STRIPE) —

Broiled Striper Fillets

2	pounds fresh striper or hybrid fillets
⅓	cup orange juice
1	tablespoon soy sauce
1	teaspoon salt
	Dash of pepper
½	stick butter or margarine, melted

Preheat the oven to broil. Cut the fillets into serving-size portions. Mix the orange juice, soy sauce, salt, pepper, and butter. Place the fish in a greased broiler pan, and brush the fillets with the sauce. Broil 3 inches from the heat source for 4 to 5 minutes with occasional basting. Turn carefully and brush with sauce. Broil again 4 to 5 minutes with occasional basting. The fish is done when flaky.

MAKES 3 TO 6 SERVINGS.

Sautéed Stripe

Gary Lee
Nashville, Tennessee

You made a reference in your column in the Banner *to stripe's not being your favorite fish to eat. I don't care for them fried either, but on a weekend trip to Lake Barkley, a friend showed me a way to cook them that is very tasty. Sorry I don't have any exact measurements in the recipe but it's not hard to just kind of eyeball it. This is really good served over rice. You can also fix this recipe in the oven, but it seems to taste better on a grill, especially if you have one that you can close the top on for a few minutes. I hope you try it. It may change your mind about the flavor of stripe.* —GARY LEE

Bell peppers

Onion

Garlic

Olive oil

Stripe fillets

Lea & Perrins White Wine Worcestershire Sauce

Salt and pepper

Paprika

Lemon or lime juice

Melted butter

Take an aluminum pan (like rolls come in), or make one out of heavy aluminum foil, big enough to fit on a grill. Slice some bell peppers, onions, and a few cloves of garlic. Put enough olive oil in the pan to just cover the bottom, and then set it on the rack of a hot grill. Add the peppers, onions, and garlic. Sauté the vegetables for a few minutes in the oil. Add the stripe (or other fish) fillets, and continue to sauté, adding several dashes of white wine Worcestershire sauce (not too much or it will overpower the flavor). Add the pepper, salt, paprika, lemon or lime juice, and whatever else you prefer. Also add some melted butter or margarine, if you like. Cook the fish for 10 minutes or so, or until it flakes with a fork.

SERVINGS WILL DEPEND ON THE NUMBER OF FILLETS.

The best time to troll for surface-oriented stripers is during March, April, and May and also during November and December. During the rest of the year, downriggers, divers, and other deep-water techniques produce most of the fish.

Warren's Striper Surprise

Stan Warren
Bethel Springs, Tennessee

When you cut your striper fillets, make sure you remove the red meat. Cut along the grain to make 1-inch chunks.
—STAN WARREN

Shrimp and crab boil (seafood boil product like Zatarain's or Old Bay)

2 **teaspoons lemon juice**

1 **tablespoon salt**

2 **pounds striper, cut into 1-inch chunks**

Jalapeños (optional)

Mushrooms (optional)

Various kinds of peppers (optional)

Onion (optional)

Olive halves (optional)

Sliced squash (optional)

Bacon slices (optional)

Italian dressing (optional)

Small red potatoes (optional)

Corn on the cob (optional)

Boil the shrimp and crab boil with the lemon juice and salt for 10 minutes. Add the striper chunks, and cook them for 2 minutes. Allow the chunks to sit for at least 5 minutes after removing from the heat. Remove, drain, and chill. The chunks are good with cocktail sauce right then. Take the chilled chunks, and add slices of jalapeños, mushrooms, or any other optional ingredients; wrap them in thin slices of the bacon. Pin the wraps with toothpicks, baste with Italian dressing, and put on a hot grill until the bacon is crispy. To really dress things up, save the shrimp/crab boil, and cook small red potatoes and corn on the cob in it while the main dish is grilling. Serve with large bibs.

MAKES 4 TO 6 SERVINGS.

— BLACK BASS —

Zesty Bass

1	cup finely chopped onion
1	cup chopped parsley
2	tablespoons olive oil or peanut oil
1	tablespoon finely chopped garlic
4	cups peeled and chopped fresh tomatoes
	Ground red pepper
2	cups burgundy wine
1	tablespoon soy sauce
	Salt and pepper
4	(5- to 8-ounce) bass fillets with skin

Place the onions and parsley in the oil, and sauté 3 to 5 minutes. Add the garlic, tomatoes, red pepper, wine, and soy sauce. Cook until the onions are translucent, about 10 minutes. Lightly season the fillets with salt and pepper to taste. Place them, skin side up, on a medium-hot grill for 3 minutes. Turn and cook 2 minutes more. Place on aluminum foil in a grill-safe pan on the grill; top with sauce. Close the top of the grill, and cook 10 minutes.

MAKES 4 SERVINGS.

To keep scent on crankbaits, replace the front hooks with a baitkeeper treble hook, the kind catfish anglers use when fishing with stinkbaits. This hook style has a little spring wrapped around the shank. Pack the spring with Berkley Power Nuggets or panfish attractant. This solid scent lasts much longer than scent sprayed on the bait, and the modified hook doesn't affect the action of the lure.

WEAR YOUR LIFE JACKET

For more than 25 years, I've signed off my fishing and hunting show with the phrase, "Wear your life jacket." My reason for closing *The Tennessee Outdoorsmen Show* with this phrase came about after I had a near fatal accident on Kentucky Lake. I dang near became paranoid about wearing life jackets and checking steering connections on outboard engines.

The accident happened late one afternoon when Harvey Mastin, a tournament fisherman, and I had been testing the waters of Trace Creek. It was getting late and we needed to return to Trail's End Resort for the Professional Bass Angler's tournament drawing. Leaving Trace Creek, Harvey opened the throttle on his 16-foot Astroglass boat powered by a 115-horsepower engine. The take-off was as smooth as a mirror. The boat planed off and was riding beautifully. Then I felt the boat fishtail. I looked over at Harvey, and he said, "We've lost the steering!"

I grabbed a handrail on the port side of the boat. Harvey eased back on the throttle, and the boat shot like a bullet to the left at almost 90 degrees. I saw Harvey leave the boat. I held onto the handrail as long as I could. The next thing I recall is opening my eyes; I was underwater but wearing my life jacket. I believe I was knocked unconscious. The next thing I knew, I was on the surface looking for Harvey and the boat. I spotted the boat circling around and around about 30 yards away. Harvey was about 50 yards downstream and he had his life jacket on. We shouted to each other to make sure neither was injured. We reached each other in a few minutes and watched as the boat engine roared loudly and the boat continued to circle. We got as far away from that boat as possible.

Just how long we floated out in the middle of Kentucky Lake I don't know. Later a boat eased up to Harvey and me, and we got in. To this day, I cannot remember the man's name who picked us up, but God bless him!

My son, Denny, came in the motor home and saw me laying everything out to dry and asked what had happened. I told him and his eyes were as big as saucers. When I was reaching for some dry pants, I turned my back to my son and he asked, "What on earth happened to your back?" I looked into the closet-door mirror. My back was black and blue from just below my shoulder down to my bottom. Evidently, my back had struck the engine when I was thrown from the boat. I truly consider myself a very lucky man to be here today after that accident.

We went back and got the boat after it had run out of fuel. Checking the engine, we found the steering control nut had backed off its connection to the steering arm, so we could not steer the boat.

Again, I thank God I was wearing my life jacket. From that day on, I've always said at the end of *The Tennessee Outdoorsmen Show*, "Wear your life jacket."

Slightly Fancy Fried Bass

I prefer crappie, but if I have only bass, here's what I do to make it taste more like crappie.
—VERN

1½ **pounds bass fillets**

¼ **teaspoon salt**

⅛ **teaspoon pepper**

½ **cup flour**

2 **tablespoons butter or margarine**

1 **cup sliced fresh mushrooms**

¼ **cup sliced green onions**

2 **tablespoons dry white wine**

1 **tablespoon lemon juice**

Sprinkle the fillets with salt and pepper, and then dredge them lightly in the flour. Melt the butter over medium heat. Fry the fillets until brown on both sides, and remove them to a plate, keeping them warm. Add more butter to the skillet, and add the mushrooms and green onions. Cook them for about 3 minutes. Stir in the wine and lemon juice. Pour this mixture over the fish and serve. Sprinkle extra onions over the top.

MAKES 3 TO 4 SERVINGS.

Orange Bass

Ellen Bilodeau
Scottsville, Kentucky

Bass fillets

Orange juice

Garlic salt

All-purpose flour

Oil for frying

In the refrigerator, soak the fillets in a mixture of orange juice and garlic salt overnight, or all day. Turn the fillets once during soaking. Drain the juice from the fillets. Coat the fillets with the flour, and fry in the oil.

SERVINGS WILL DEPEND ON THE NUMBER OF FILLETS.

Bass-Stuffed Mushroom Caps

1 (8-ounce) bass fillet

6 tablespoons sour cream

1 teaspoon curry powder

½ teaspoon salt

Pinch of cayenne

1 rib celery, diced

4 green onions, diced

16 (2-inch diameter) mushrooms

2 tablespoons melted butter

Cook the bass fillet in the microwave. Chill for 30 to 60 minutes, and then flake. Stir together the sour cream, curry powder, salt, and cayenne. Fold in the diced celery, onions, and flaked fish. Cover and refrigerate. Preheat the oven to 375 degrees. Remove the mushroom stems. Rinse the caps and dry. Set on a lightly oiled baking sheet. Brush the mushrooms with the melted butter, and then add a dollop of the bass mixture. Bake for 15 minutes.

MAKES 2 SERVINGS.

— BREAM —

When the English landed in North America, they found a fish that resembled their bream back home. The two fish are not related, but the English name has stuck on the American fish for several centuries. I guess we'll live with it a little longer.

Bream are a member of the sunfish family, which also includes the black basses. Tennessee has 20 bream varieties, but only about 9 are commonly caught. Although the two largest bream, the bluegill and shellcracker, are the most sought after, all bream have a sweet, mild taste.

Lemon Fried Bluegill

Ellen Bilodeau
Scottsville, Kentucky

1	cup all-purpose flour, plus additional flour for dredging
2	teaspoons grated lemon peel
½	teaspoon salt
¼	teaspoon pepper
1	cup water
	Vegetable oil (for frying)
1½	pounds bluegill
	All-purpose flour

Blend the 1 cup flour, the lemon peel, salt, and pepper. Add the water, mix, and chill for 30 minutes. Heat 2 inches of oil in a fryer to 375 degrees. Coat the fish in additional flour, and dip in the batter. Fry for about 3 minutes. Drain on paper towels.

MAKES 4 TO 6 SERVINGS.

Peanut Panfish Dip

Ellen Bilodeau
Scottsville, Kentucky

1	pound cooked, flaked bluegill
1	cup sour cream
¼	cup peanut dust (peanuts crushed in a blender), plus additional for sprinkling
1	tablespoon fresh lemon juice
3	tablespoons minced onion
¼	teaspoon salt

Combine the fish, sour cream, peanut dust, lemon juice, onion, and salt; chill. Serve sprinkled with additional peanut dust.

MAKES 2 CUPS.

Cocktail Bream

8   bream
    Salt
    Cocktail sauce

Place the whole fish in boiling water for 6 minutes. Remove from the water, and peel the white meat from the bone. Salt to taste. Chill thoroughly, and serve with your favorite cocktail sauce.

MAKES 4 SERVINGS.

— SAUGER AND WALLEYE —

Orange Sauger or Walleye

Bridget Stensgard
Oronoco, Minnesota

    Butter or margarine
4   walleye or other firm fish
    fillets
1   orange, quartered
    Sesame seeds
    Garlic powder
    Onion powder
    Parsley
    Parmesan cheese (optional)

Preheat the oven to 425 degrees. Rub the bottom of a glass baking dish with a small amount of butter or margarine. Lay the fillets in one layer in the dish. Squeeze 2 or 3 orange quarters over the fish; then sprinkle the sesame seeds, garlic powder, onion powder, and parsley over the top. Sprinkle a little Parmesan cheese over the top if desired. Bake for 10 to 15 minutes, or until the fish flakes easily with a fork.

MAKES 4 SERVINGS.

Use finesse tactics for inactive sauger and walleye, or when the water is very clear.

Jig color depends on water clarity. Brighter colors like orange, pink, lime green, and chartreuse are good in dingy water. Clear water calls for more subtle hues like crawdad, smoke, and dark greens.

Sauger/Walleye with Rice Stuffing

Bridget Stensgard
Oronoco, Minnesota

I got this recipe from a fishing buddy's wife when I lived in Minnesota. I was a south Alabama boy who didn't know what a walleye was. When I moved to Tennessee in the late 1960s, I gave away the first ones I caught below Cheatham Dam, because they looked too ugly to eat. —VERN

1 **(6-ounce package) wild and long grain rice mix**

1 **teaspoon instant chicken bouillon granules**

½ **cup sliced fresh mushrooms (optional)**

½ **cup chopped celery**

2 **tablespoons butter**

1 **(2-ounce) jar drained, sliced pimiento**

⅛ **teaspoon ground sage**

2 to 2½ **pounds sauger or walleye**

Preheat the oven to 375 degrees. Prepare the rice as directed on the package, adding the bouillon granules to the water. Grease a broiler pan or 13 x 9-inch baking pan. In a small skillet, cook and stir the mushrooms and celery in the butter over medium heat until the mushrooms are tender, about 5 minutes. Stir in the pimiento and sage. Stir the vegetables into the rice. Place the fish on the broiler pan. Stuff with the rice mixture, placing any extra stuffing around the fish. Cover only the rice with foil. Bake until the fish flakes easily at the backbone, 20 to 25 minutes.

MAKES 4 TO 6 SERVINGS.

Lemon Pepper Sauger

I forgot where I got this one, but it will also work with walleye, catfish, bass, and crappie.

—VERN

4 sauger fillets

1 cup Lawry's Lemon Pepper with Lemon Juice Marinade

1 cup bread crumbs

½ teaspoon seasoned salt

½ teaspoon lemon pepper

2 tablespoons vegetable oil

2 tablespoons butter or margarine

⅓ cup light cream or half-and-half

1 tablespoon grated lemon rind

⅓ cup toasted sliced almonds

In a resealable plastic bag or container, place the fillets and the Lemon Pepper with Lemon Juice Marinade. Marinate in the refrigerator for 30 minutes. In a shallow pan, combine the bread crumbs, seasoned salt, and lemon pepper, mixing well. Remove the fillets from the marinade, and roll in the bread crumb mixture until completely covered. In a large fry pan, heat the oil and butter. Add the fillets, and cook for 3 to 4 minutes on each side, or until golden brown and the fish flakes easily. Remove to a serving platter, and keep warm. Add the cream and grated lemon rind to the pan drippings, and bring to a boil. Stir constantly until slightly thickened. Spoon the sauce over the fillets, and sprinkle with the almonds.

MAKES 4 SERVINGS.

Potato-Coated Sauger or Walleye

Bridget Stensgard
Oronoco, Minnesota

½ cup all-purpose flour

1 teaspoon paprika

½ teaspoon salt

¼ teaspoon pepper

Garlic powder

Parsley

1 cup instant potato flakes

1½ pounds sauger/walleye fillets

2 beaten eggs

Oil for frying

Lemon wedges

Tartar sauce

Combine the flour, paprika, salt, pepper, garlic powder, and parsley in a shallow bowl. Put the potato flakes on a plate. Dredge the fillets in the flour mixture, dip them in the eggs, and then roll in the potato flakes. Heat about ½ inch of oil in a large skillet. Fry the fillets 2 to 3 minutes per side, until golden brown, and drain on a paper-towel-covered plate. Serve with lemon wedges and/or tartar sauce.

MAKES 4 TO 5 SERVINGS.

Markham's Pretzeled Sauger

Vernon Summerlin
Leipers Fork, Tennessee

My buddy Doug Markham left a bag of pretzels in my boat after a fishing trip. Rather than throw them away, I used them in a recipe to replace flour. —VERN

2 cups pretzels

1 cup instant potatoes

Pinch of thyme

1 egg

¼ cup milk

1 teaspoon lime juice

4 to 6 sauger fillets

Oil for frying

Roll the pretzels and instant potatoes to a fine powder, and mix with thyme in a resealable bag. Mix the egg, milk, and lime juice in a medium bowl. Dip the fillets in the mixture, and then shake the fillets in the pretzel-potato mixture bag. Fry in 375-degree oil in a heavy iron skillet, or until done, 2 to 3 minutes.

MAKES 4 TO 6 SERVINGS.

Summerlin's Sauger Cocktail

Cathy Summerlin
Leipers Fork, Tennessee

I revamped a saltwater fish recipe to use sauger. Crappie would make a good substitute, but sauger is my first choice. —CATHY SUMMERLIN

Salt

1 tablespoon lemon juice

1 pound bite-sized sauger pieces

Iced water

Seafood cocktail sauce

Place the salt and lemon juice in water in a 3-quart pan and bring to a boil. Reduce the heat to medium, and add the fish pieces. Cook for several minutes, until the fish is opaque and beginning to curl up. Remove the fish, and drop it into the iced water. When the fish has cooled completely, drain and serve with cocktail sauce as you would shrimp.

MAKES 4 TO 6 SERVINGS AS AN APPETIZER.

Store several gallon-size, plastic, resealable bags in your tackle box to bring home your cleaned fish in.

— GAR —

Vern told me this story about a time he went fishing for gar with the intention of making gar balls: "When I finally landed a 2½-footer, I didn't have the tools to fillet it— my fillet knife wasn't strong enough. One friend said use tin snips, another said a hatchet, and another said a chain saw. I let the unharmed gar go, and I've yet to find an easy way to fillet gar."

Gar Stew

Oil for frying
5 pounds gar or catfish
½ pound diced bacon
3 pounds diced red potatoes
2 pounds diced white onions
5 cups water
6 diced hard-cooked eggs
1 (6-ounce) can evaporated milk
Salt and pepper

Fry the fish in hot oil until flaky, using a batter recipe of cornmeal, milk, and seasonings. Fry the bacon until crisp, and remove from the skillet. Fry the potatoes and onions in the bacon drippings until tender. Place the fish in 4 cups of the water in a cast iron Dutch oven. Add the bacon, potatoes, onions, and eggs. Simmer for 1 to 1½ hours, adding the remaining water if needed. Add the milk, stirring constantly; season with salt and pepper.

MAKES 8 TO 10 SERVINGS.

Gar Nuggets

Carl and Ellen Ruehling
Altamont, Tennessee

We saw you joke about gar balls on your show. Once you try my gar nuggets, I think you'll think differently about them. Gar nuggets can be served as a snack, appetizer, or main dish. They are good dipped in barbecue sauce, honey, mustard sauce, or sweet-and-sour sauce.
—ELLEN RUEHLING

2½ **pounds gar fillets, cut in 1-inch squares**

Salt

Lemon pepper

Buttermilk

1 **cup self-rising flour**

Oil for frying

Place the gar pieces in a small bowl, and sprinkle with the salt and lemon pepper to taste. Cover with the buttermilk, and let sit in the refrigerator for 2 to 3 hours. Coat the pieces with the flour after draining off the buttermilk, and deep-fry in the oil until golden brown.

MAKES 6 TO 8 SERVINGS.

It's easy to become overwhelmed while trying to find fish on large bodies of water. You'll catch more fish if you break down big lakes into manageable sections and dissect the smaller sections thoroughly. The trick is to select a section of the lake that is likely to hold the fish you want to catch at the season you are fishing, and take your time, approaching the section like it's a small lake unto itself.

Chapter 2

Bait-Stealing Turtles

Snappers and Other Tasty Shellbacks

Catching the turtle is up to you. Some people catch turtles with their bare hands along lakes, rivers, or roadsides. They can also be caught on a hook covered with meat. Once you catch one, cut its head off, letting the blood drain. Be careful with the head. It can still cause a nasty bite long after it has been severed. Here's how to clean a snapping turtle: Cut around the edge of the bottom shell, and cut through the joint between the top and bottom shell on each side. The bottom shell will lift out. Remove the insides and discard. Cut the legs and neck loose from the inside of the top shell. Remove the skin from the legs and neck. You can parboil or pressure-cook the turtle meat to make it tender before using it in a recipe.

Here's another way to clean a turtle: Scrub the decapitated turtle with laundry soap and a stiff brush until it is clean. Place the turtle in a pot large enough to hold the whole turtle for boiling. Boil the whole turtle for 30 to 40 minutes. Take the pot outside, pour the turtle on the grass, and leave it until the turtle is cool enough to handle. You can use the sink if you prefer. Turn the turtle upside down and cut out the under shell. There are seven different flavors of turtle meat. The choicest lies along the backbone; and without boiling the turtle first, it is almost impossible to get this meat out. I then toss the good meat into one pan and the discards into the other. Muscle meat is good, but the fat isn't so good. Find the liver; it is excellent, but the gall bladder must be cut away and discarded.

You can fry turtle like chicken, or use it for soup.

Pretty Good Turtle Stew

Cubed meat from one medium-size turtle

1 large onion, chopped

2 to 3 garlic cloves, cubed

Oil

4 to 5 potatoes, cubed

2 (14 ½-ounce) cans peeled tomatoes, or 8 to 10 fresh tomatoes, coarsely chopped

1 (12-ounce) can corn, or 1 package frozen corn

Salt and pepper

Garlic powder

Whole wheat flour (optional)

Brown the turtle meat with the onion and garlic in a hot skillet with a little cooking oil (get the skillet really hot, and drop the pieces of meat into the hot oil). When the meat is browned on all sides, drain the oil and transfer the meat, onions, and garlic to a Dutch oven. Add the potatoes, tomatoes, and corn. Season the mixture with salt, pepper, and garlic powder to taste. Add water to just cover the ingredients, and cook, covered, at a high simmer for 45 minutes, or until the potatoes are thoroughly cooked. The stew is ready to eat; however, some cooks prefer to thicken the stew with a whole-wheat flour/water mixture. If you do this, you should simmer the mixture for another 15 minutes.

MAKES 4 TO 6 SERVINGS.

Most 35 mm film comes in canisters that make good containers for hooks, lead sinkers, small jigs, and the like.

Turtle Chowder

A. J. Hayes
Deceased owner of Cove Hollow Resort on Center Hill Lake, Lancaster, Tennessee

1	snapping turtle
1	pound bacon
6	medium potatoes, chopped
3	medium onions, chopped
1	cup chopped celery
4	carrots, chopped
1	cup chopped broccoli
1	(16-ounce) can cream-style corn
2	tablespoons Worcestershire sauce
2	tablespoons chopped parsley
1	teaspoon salt
1	teaspoon pepper

Chop the turtle meat into small cubes. Combine with the bacon in a saucepan, and fry until the bacon is crisp, stirring to brown turtle meat. Remove the bacon. Add enough water to the turtle meat and drippings to cover by about 3 inches. Add the potatoes, onions, celery, carrots, broccoli, corn, Worcestershire sauce, parsley, salt, and pepper. Simmer, covered, for 3 hours. Chill overnight, and reheat for best flavor. Ladle into soup bowls, crumble bacon over the top of the chowder, and serve.

MAKES 4 TO 6 SERVINGS.

Creamed Terrapin

2	tablespoons butter
1	tablespoon flour
1	pint cream
1	teaspoon salt
1	teaspoon white pepper
1	teaspoon grated nutmeg
	Pinch of cayenne
1	pint terrapin meat
4	eggs, beaten
4	ounces good sherry (optional)
1	tablespoon lemon juice

In the top of a double boiler, mix the butter and flour, and gradually stir in the cream, salt, white pepper, nutmeg, cayenne, and terrapin meat. Heat and stir all until scalding hot. Place over a pan of hot water, where the contents will keep hot, but will not boil. Then stir in the eggs, but do not allow the terrapin to boil after adding the eggs. Just before serving, add sherry and lemon juice.

MAKES 4 TO 6 SERVINGS.

Chapter 3

Small Feathered Game

Quail, Dove, Pheasant, Grouse

— HOW I LEARNED TO COOK WILD GAME —

Through the years, people have asked me when and where my interest in cooking started. I can tell you: when I began hunting with Amon Carter Evans, former owner of the Nashville *Tennessean* newspaper, in West Sandy Wildlife Management Area in West Tennessee, near Paris. Most hunters know West Sandy WMA as Springville Bottoms. Amon and I hunted together there for twenty years or more.

Anyway, I knew a little bit about cooking. I could cook up a great mess of fish, hush puppies, and coleslaw with a big, heaping tablespoon or two of white beans.

But Amon could cook 'most anything. He is truly a chef and can cook with the best. I watched Amon prepare meals at the duck camp there in Springville Bottoms. I would ask him questions about how he prepared certain meals, and he would tell me. I had my pen in hand and wrote everything down. For instance, when Amon and I cooked steaks or wild game on a charcoal grill, the coals had to be just right. He liked to sear the meats, telling me this sealed in the flavor.

Over the years I've learned to cook all kinds of wild game and waterfowl. I must admit, though, I've never been able to cook a goose. I've never eaten any goose that I liked.

I've also learned how important it is to properly clean, wash, and store wild game. If I freeze game, after cleaning and washing it, I put it in a plastic freezer bag or a milk carton. You can use a coffee can with a plastic lid, too. Just pack the wild meat or fish into the can, add water, and freeze.

— QUAIL —

Baked Quail

William and Andrea Bolden
Unionville, Tennessee

3 tablespoons butter

1 teaspoon lemon juice

½ cup ginger ale

6 to 8 quail

Preheat the oven to 350 degrees. Heat the butter, lemon juice, and ginger ale over low heat until the butter melts. Place the quail in the baking dish, pour the ginger ale mixture over the birds, and bake in the oven for 30 minutes, basting frequently.

MAKES 6 TO 8 SERVINGS.

Baked Quail with Wine

Mrs. H. S. Stinson
Old Hickory, Tennessee

4 quail

1 cup flour

   Salt and pepper

1 cup butter

1 cup white cooking wine

1 (14 ½ -ounce) can
   chicken broth

Preheat the oven to 250 to 300 degrees. Shake the quail in a paper bag with the flour, and salt and pepper to taste. Brown the floured birds in butter in a large ovenproof skillet. Add the wine and chicken broth, and stir to blend. Cover and bake in the oven for 1 to 2 hours. Serve with rice.

MAKES 4 SERVINGS.

You can locate quail by looking for scratching spots and roosting areas. Quail roost in a circle and leave their droppings in that design. Fresh droppings are soft and indicate birds are in that area.

Cognac Quail

Mildred Curle
Nashville, Tennessee

4 to 6 quail

8   shallots, chopped

4   tablespoons butter

¹⁄₂ cup cognac

2   cups chicken broth

1   cup whipping cream
    Salt and pepper

Preheat the oven to 350 degrees. In a heavy skillet on the stovetop, brown the quail with the shallots in butter. Pour the cognac over the quail, and stir lightly over low heat until the cognac evaporates. Place the quail and the shallots in an oven dish, and cover with the chicken broth. Cook in the oven 30 minutes. Pour the whipping cream over the quail, and serve with wild rice, using the gravy from the oven dish.

MAKES 4 TO 6 SERVINGS.

Quail or Grouse Supreme

Auda Eldridge
Nashville, Tennessee

3   quail or 1 grouse

¹⁄₂ teaspoon poultry seasoning

2   tablespoons chopped onion

**1   tablespoon chopped green
    pepper**

¹⁄₄ cup chopped mushrooms
    Salt and pepper

¹⁄₂ teaspoon sage

2   slices bacon

Soak the quail or grouse in salted water for 1 hour in the refrigerator. Dry thoroughly. Preheat the oven to 375 degrees. Combine the poultry seasoning, onion, green pepper, mushrooms, salt, pepper, and sage. Stuff the birds with the mixture, and truss with poultry skewers. Wrap the birds with bacon. Place any leftover stuffing on the birds, cover, and roast in the oven for 1 hour, or until browned.

MAKES 3 SERVINGS.

Quail and Mushrooms

Randy Lochridge

6 slices bacon

6 quail

Salt and pepper

½ pound mushroom caps

1 bunch green onions

3 tablespoons melted butter

2 tablespoons prepared mustard

¼ teaspoon dry ginger

1 cup orange marmalade

Preheat the oven to 325 degrees. Wrap the bacon around the birds, and arrange in rows on a large sheet of heavy-duty aluminum foil. Season with salt and pepper to taste. Sauté the mushrooms and green onions in the butter, and pour over the quail. Seal with a double wrap of foil, and bake for 1 hour. Combine the mustard, ginger, and marmalade, and pour over quail to serve.

MAKES 6 SERVINGS.

Quickie Quail

6 quail breasts

Seasoning salt

Pepper

Bacon

Preheat the oven to 375 degrees. Place the quail breasts in a baking pan, and sprinkle with seasoning salt and pepper. Place half a slice of bacon around each quail breast. Bake, covered, for 20 minutes, and then remove the cover and brown.

MAKES 6 SERVINGS.

The "bob-white" whistle of early spring is an indication that the quail coveys are beginning to break up and individual males and females are beginning their courtship behavior. An adult hen and cock quail will usually pair off for the entire nesting season.

Fried Quail

Otis Henry
Franklin, Tennessee

As many quail as required

Salt and pepper

All-purpose flour

Cooking oil or lard for frying

Paprika

Dress each quail, and split it down the back, leaving the halves attached. Season both sides of each bird with salt and pepper to taste. Put the birds into a bag with the flour, and shake to cover all parts. Remove quail from the bag, and flatten them in hot oil (or lard) with the breasts down, using enough oil so that the birds are at least half immersed. Turn birds until well browned on both sides, and then cover them and reduce the heat. Cook an additional 30 minutes or until tender, adding a little water or other liquid if necessary. Sprinkle with the paprika. Thicken the pan liquid with a paste of flour and water to make the gravy.

SERVINGS WILL DEPEND ON THE NUMBER OF QUAIL COOKED.

— DOVE —

Grilled Dove Breasts

6   **dove breasts**

Bacon

Salt and pepper

Your favorite seasonings

Wrap the dove breasts with strips of the bacon. Salt, pepper, and season to taste. Place on a gas, charcoal, or electric burner; grill until tender.

MAKES 4 TO 6 SERVINGS.

Smothered Doves

1 stick butter

2 tablespoons all-purpose flour

2 cups water

Salt and pepper

1 tablespoon Worcestershire sauce

2 tablespoons lemon juice

6 doves

Preheat the oven to 350 degrees. Melt the butter in a skillet. Add the flour, and cook until smooth and brown. Add water gradually, stirring well until thickened. Stir in salt, pepper, Worcestershire sauce, and lemon juice. Arrange the doves in a baking dish; pour the sauce over the doves and cover the dish. Bake in the oven for 2 hours. Baste occasionally, and add water if necessary.

MAKES 4 TO 6 SERVINGS.

Roast Doves

Mildred Curle
Nashville, Tennessee

Be careful with Mildred's flaming cognac. —JIMMY

Salt and pepper

12 doves

24 juniper berries

1 stick butter

¼ cup cognac

Preheat the oven to 350 degrees. Salt and pepper the doves to taste, and place 2 juniper berries inside each. In a heavy, ovenproof skillet, brown the birds with the butter. Cover the skillet, and bake in the oven for 30 minutes. Remove from the oven and uncover. In a ladle, warm the cognac, ignite it, and pour over the birds.

MAKES 6 TO 8 SERVINGS.

Doves entering and leaving a feeding field often use certain flyways. Look for these flight lines, and be prepared to move into position as the doves' flight dictates.

Dove or Quail Casserole

6 doves or quail
Butter or margarine

1   (32-ounce) carton sour
    cream
1   (10¾-ounce) can condensed
    cream of mushroom soup

Preheat the oven to 350 degrees. Brown the birds in butter, and save the drippings. Place the birds in a greased, 1-quart casserole dish. Mix the remaining ingredients with drippings, and pour over the browned birds. Cook, covered, for 1¼ hours.

MAKES 4 TO 6 SERVINGS.

Tipsy Doves

Joe Hughes

This recipe is delicious with dove, pheasant, or quail.   —JOE HUGHES

18 dove breasts, or breasts with
    legs
1   teaspoon salt
1   bay leaf
2   (10¾-ounce) cans
    condensed cream of
    mushroom or cream of
    chicken soup
1   cup water
1   cup chopped onion
1   tablespoon dried parsley
1   teaspoon celery seeds
1   cup sliced fresh mushrooms
1   cup white wine

Place the dove breasts in a large skillet, and barely cover with water. Add salt to taste and the bay leaf. Simmer for 20 minutes, turning once. Drain, remove, and discard the bay leaf. Combine the soup and 1 cup water in a large bowl, and stir to mix. Add the onion, parsley, and celery seeds. Mix well, and pour over the doves. Heat to simmer, cover, and simmer for 30 minutes. Add fresh mushrooms, stir, and simmer an additional 10 minutes. Add wine, and stir to mix. Heat to simmer, and serve at once. For best results, use fresh mushrooms, and do not overcook them after adding the wine.

MAKES 4 TO 6 SERVINGS.

Souped Up Doves

Pauline Wells
Camden, Tennessee

The soup makes an excellent gravy to pour over the meat. You can also serve it as a side dish. —PAULINE WELLS

6	**dove breasts**
	Salt and pepper
	All-purpose flour
	Oil
1	**(10 ¾-ounce) can condensed cream of mushroom soup**

Cut the meat from the dove breasts. Salt and pepper to taste, and dust with flour. Brown in oil. When lightly browned on both sides, pour soup and a soup can of water over the meat; simmer until tender.

MAKES 4 TO 6 SERVINGS.

Braised Doves in Wine

Edna and Emmett Webb
Nashville, Tennessee

My mother-in-law, Ann Webb, who has passed away, gave this recipe to me. My husband says this is the best dove recipe. Add more wine if you want more gravy. I transfer the doves to a long ceramic baking dish for serving. —EDNA WEBB

	Salt and pepper
6	**doves**
	All-purpose flour
½	**cup oil**
1	**cup white wine**

Salt and pepper the doves to taste, and coat lightly with flour. Heat the oil in a Dutch oven or deep skillet, and brown the doves. Add water to cover the doves halfway. Add the wine, and cook for 1 hour.

MAKES 4 TO 6 SERVINGS.

Dove, Quail, Snipe, or Woodcock Amandine

12 doves, quail, or snipes, or 6 woodcock, split down the back

¼ cup all-purpose flour

Salt and pepper

4 tablespoons butter

½ cup white table wine

2 teaspoons lemon juice

¼ cup blanched, sliced almonds

Dust the birds in flour seasoned with salt and pepper to taste. Melt the butter in a heavy skillet or electric frying pan, and sauté the birds until nicely browned. Add wine and lemon juice. Cover and continue cooking slowly for 15 to 20 minutes. Add almonds, and cook for 5 to 10 minutes longer, or until birds are fork tender.

MAKES 6 SERVINGS.

— PHEASANT —

Pheasant Rice Bake

1 pheasant, cut in pieces

Vinegar or lemon juice

1 package onion soup mix

1 cup rice

1 (10¾-ounce) can condensed cream of mushroom soup

1 soup can of milk

1 (8-ounce) can French fried onion rings

Simmer the pheasant in water with a small amount of the vinegar or lemon juice to help tenderize the bird. Preheat the oven to 350 degrees. Sprinkle the dry soup mix into a buttered casserole dish. Sprinkle the rice over the soup mix. Add the cooked pheasant pieces. Mix the soup and milk, and pour the mixture over the pheasant. Cover and bake in the oven for 1¼ hours. Uncover and sprinkle with the onion rings. Cook 15 minutes longer.

MAKES 4 TO 6 SERVINGS.

Male pheasant are highly colored with a white neck ring and long tail. Female pheasant are brown and have a long tail also.

South of the Border Pheasant

2 cups cooked pheasant, cut in 1-inch pieces

1 (10³/₄-ounce) can condensed cream of mushroom soup

1 (10³/₄-ounce) can condensed cream of chicken soup

½ cup chopped onion

1 cup salsa

1 cup sour cream

2 cups Monterey Jack or cheddar cheese

1 package corn tortillas, cut in strips

1 jalapeño pepper, finely chopped (optional)

Preheat the oven to 350 degrees. Combine the pheasant, soups, onion, salsa, sour cream, and 1½ cups of the cheese. Layer the mixture with the tortilla strips. Top with the remaining ¼ cup cheese and the jalapeño. Bake in the oven for 30 minutes.

MAKES 6 TO 8 SERVINGS.

Pheasant with Wild Rice

*This recipe is from Meadow Brook Game Farm. The owners give one to each customer
who takes pheasant.*   —JIMMY

2   **pheasant (may be cut in
    halves)**

3   **cups water**

    Salt

3 to 4 tablespoons cornstarch

½   **(10¾-ounce) can condensed
    cream of mushroom soup**

½   **(10¾-ounce) can condensed
    cream of celery soup**

½   **(10¾-ounce) can condensed
    cream of chicken soup**

1   **(8-ounce) box wild rice**

Soak the pheasant in water for several hours in
the refrigerator before cooking. Put the birds in
a large pot, add the water and salt to taste, and
heat to a hard boil. Skim the surface if needed.
Reduce the heat, and cook slowly until tender.
Remove the birds and cool. Strain the broth to
remove the bone fragments if present. Return
the broth to the pot, and add the cornstarch
dissolved in cold water. Add the mushroom,
celery, and chicken soups to the broth. Remove
the meat from the bones, and add it to the
broth. Simmer for 30 minutes. Cook the rice as
directed on the box; serve the pheasant with, or
on, a bed of rice.

MAKES 4 TO 6 SERVINGS.

You'll flush more birds by walking slowly
and quietly and working back and forth
across the field. This forces the bird to
either flush or move ahead of the walkers,
giving blockers at the end of the cover an
opportunity for a shot.

Pheasant Pasta

Gary Gillispie
Nashville, Tennessee

I've made this dish many times. It's easy and delicious. Serve it with a green vegetable or hearty salad.
—GARY GILLISPIE

1   **cup sour cream**

1   **cup heavy cream**

1   **pheasant breast, diced into $\frac{1}{2}$-inch cubes**

2   **tablespoons butter**

1   **cup diced ham**

2   **(6-ounce) cans tomato paste**

$\frac{1}{2}$ **teaspoon lemon-pepper seasoning**

1   **teaspoon Italian seasoning**

$\frac{1}{2}$ **teaspoon pepper**

$\frac{1}{4}$ **teaspoon salt**

  Pinch of dry, crushed red pepper flakes

1   **pound pasta or rice**

Mix the sour cream and heavy cream in a small bowl, and refrigerate for 4 to 6 hours. Brown the breast cubes in a skillet with the melted butter over medium heat. Add the diced ham, and cook about 5 minutes. Stir in the tomato paste, lemon-pepper seasoning, Italian seasoning, pepper, salt, and red pepper flakes. Lower the heat, and simmer 10 minutes. Add the sour cream mixture, and cook until heated, stirring constantly. Cook the pasta or rice according to package directions. Serve the sauce over the cooked pasta or rice.

MAKES 2 TO 3 SERVINGS.

Ground Pheasant

Pheasant trimmings

Beef fat

Oil

Save the meat from the thighs, back, and upper drumsticks of the pheasant, and freeze in airtight containers (should yield 8 to 10 ounces per bird). Parts can be included, such as shot-up breast pieces of pheasant, quail, or ruffed grouse. When you have accumulated a supply of meat, grind with beef fat at about 4 to 5 parts pheasant with 1 part fat. For a low-fat, low-cholesterol version, add 1 to 2 tablespoons of cooking oil instead of fat. The ground meat can be used for patties, meat loaf, hamburger steak, and hamburger gravies. It will work well for anything that calls for pork sausage.

SERVINGS WILL DEPEND ON AMOUNT OF GAME SAVED.

— GROUSE —

Hunter's Grouse

Fred Scarbrough
Mufreesboro, Tennessee

3   **tablespoons butter**

2   **grouse**

   Salt and pepper

1   **pint white wine**

2   **cups cream**

Melt the butter in a cast iron skillet. Brown the birds on each side. Salt and pepper to taste. Preheat the oven to 375 degrees. Place the birds in a deep dish or pan, and add the white wine. Baste several times. Cover and bake for about 30 minutes. Baste several times, and then pour cream over the grouse before taking from the stove.

MAKES 4 SERVINGS.

Grouse with Red Cabbage

2   grouse

1   (10½-ounce) can red cabbage

½   pint sour cream

4   shallots, chopped

4   slices bacon

White wine for basting

Preheat the oven to 350 degrees. Stuff the birds with a mixture of the cabbage, sour cream, and shallots. Cover the breasts with the bacon. Roast in the oven for 1 hour, basting often with the wine.

MAKES 4 SERVINGS.

Woozy Grouse

I used this recipe a hunting buddy gave me when I lived in Minnesota. He suggests you set aside enough wine for the recipe before you start transferring wine to your glass.

—VERN

1   grouse, cut into pieces

All-purpose flour

2   tablespoons butter

Salt and pepper

2   tablespoons olive oil

1   cup light cream

1   cup dry red wine

½   cup fresh sliced mushrooms (optional)

Preheat the oven to 350 degrees. Cut the grouse into serving pieces, and roll the pieces in the flour. Brown in a skillet with the butter. Remove the grouse pieces, and place in a casserole. Put salt, pepper, olive oil, cream, wine, and mushrooms into a saucepan. Bring to a boil, and pour over the grouse in a casserole dish. Bake in the oven for 1 hour.

MAKES 2 SERVINGS.

Grouse are an upland bird and can be hunted in Tennessee east of I-65.

Chapter 4

Flying and Floating Birds

Duck, Goose, Coot

— DUCK —

Wild ducks usually taste like what they eat, because the flavors build up in the fat. They are at their prime just before their winter migration and at its end, when they're fat again. If the bird has plenty of pinfeathers, it's a young, more succulent duck. The plumage of older birds tends to be more colorful.

You want to leave some fat on your ducks when you clean them. However, you don't want to leave so much fat that the bird tastes like fat. Save the trimmed fat to render into the roasting pan and for frying potatoes.

The best advice I can give you on cooking wild duck is to roast it briefly, about 20 minutes, at a very high temperature—500 degrees is best—and serve it rare. Grilling is another option.

Domestic duck is usually cooked until the skin is crispy and the meat is gray and tasteless. French chefs tend to cook duck bloody rare. Somewhere in between those extremes is what I shoot for: the point where the blood still exudes its own flavor, a delectable rind of fat still lies under the skin, and the meat has a wonderful velvety texture.

Sweet sauces mask the flavor of duck, though several classic recipes do call for orange or cherry glazes. Smoked duck is an acquired taste I haven't yet acquired, not because it's a bad idea for older ducks, but because smoking compromises the flavor of something that is so naturally good.

Grilled Duck or Goose

Kevin "Bowana" Moore
Nashville, Tennessee

2	**duck breasts**
1	**cup Italian dressing (oil and vinegar style)**
	Salt and pepper
6	**slices bacon**
1	**tomato, sliced**
1	**onion, sliced**

Remove all the skin and fat from the breasts. Marinate them in a saucepan in the refrigerator with the Italian dressing for approximately 30 minutes. Remove the breasts from the saucepan, and add salt and pepper to taste. Wrap the breasts with the bacon. Place the breasts on a foil-lined cookie sheet, and cover with the sliced tomatoes and onions. Heat the grill to a medium-high temperature. Allow to cook in a covered grill until three-quarters done. Remove the breasts from the cookie sheet, and place on the grill for braising. Reduce the heat to low, and cook until the bacon is done.

MAKES 2 TO 4 SERVINGS.

Jimmy's Simple Duck Roast

1	**duck**
	Peeled and diced apples
	Chopped onion
	Salt and pepper
⅔	**cup port**
	1 teaspoon cornstarch
	Lemon juice

Preheat the oven to 450 to 500 degrees. Clean the cavity of the duck, and stuff it with the apples and chopped onion. Season with salt and pepper to taste. Place on a rack (to render the juices and fat), and roast in the oven for 20 minutes. Remove the bird and keep warm. Drain the fat from the pan; then add to the pan a mixture of the port and cornstarch. Stir to blend and thicken, season with salt and pepper and a squirt of lemon juice, and then strain into a sauce boat. Serve the duck with wild rice.

MAKES 2 OR 3 SERVINGS.

SPRINGVILLE DUCK BLIND SPECIALS

Fishing was my first love, but I learned to like waterfowl hunting very much. I had hunted rabbit and done some quail hunting, but waterfowl is a completely different ball game. I had to learn to call ducks. Luckily, my brother, Jack, taught me how to blow a duck call; once I had the calls down pat, I was thrilled when ducks responded.

As I mentioned earlier, I first became interested in cooking while helping out my old boss, Amon Evans, at the duck camp.

Amon was famous for the following Springville Special recipe. This sausage and biscuit dish isn't anything fancy; but in a duck blind, it was absolutely wonderful in the morning—it wasn't bad in the afternoons either.

AMON'S SPRINGVILLE SPECIAL

1   **lb. hot sausage**

1   **tube biscuits**

Block of Velveeta cheese

Fry the sausage, bake the biscuits, and slice the Velveeta cheese to equal the sausage patties. Just before you remove the sausage from the skillet, place the cheese on top of each sausage, and let it melt a tad. Place the cheese and sausage on the biscuits. Wrap them individually in aluminum foil. Pack the sausage and biscuits in a sack. When you get to the blind the next morning, get that charcoal stove hot, and toss the foil packets on the grill and let 'em warm.

MAKES 8 SERVINGS.

Cooking fresh duck breasts in a duck blind on a cold morning is also great and lots of fun. We would slice the duck breasts as thin as bacon strips and fry them in a skillet over a charcoal stove. Duck breast is very good in a biscuit on a cold morning.

Many folks marinate duck breasts in all kinds of wild game sauces. I prefer them sliced very thin, coated in a milk and egg wash, rolled in flour that has been salted and peppered, and fried crispy.

Springville Bottoms Roasted Duck Breast

Dr. Bill Bunros (deceased)
Hendersonville, Tennessee

4	**duck breast fillets**
8	**slices bacon**
1	**teaspoon salt**
	Black pepper
	Red pepper
	Cinnamon
1½	**sticks butter, sliced**
1	**bay leaf, crushed**
1	**tablespoon poultry seasoning**
1	**teaspoon parsley flakes**

Preheat the oven to 350 degrees. Rinse the fillets, pat dry, and wrap in the bacon. Sprinkle each breast with salt, black pepper, red pepper, and cinnamon. Arrange in a baking dish lined with a large piece of foil. Add the butter slices, and sprinkle with the bay leaf and seasonings. Seal the foil tightly, and bake 1¼ hours.

MAKES 4 SERVINGS.

Camden Bottoms Waterfowlers' Roasted Duck Breasts

3	**duck breasts**
	Flour
	Salt and pepper
	Oil
½	**cup chopped celery**
1	**onion, chopped**
¼	**pound (1 stick) butter**
1½	**teaspoons poultry seasoning**
1	**cup water**
1	**package prepared stuffing mix**

Roll the duck breasts in the flour seasoned with salt and pepper. Heat the oil in a skillet and brown the breasts. In a saucepan, cook the celery and onions in the butter. Stir in the poultry seasoning, and add the water. Stir in the prepared stuffing mix. More water may be added to make the stuffing moist. Preheat the oven to 350 degrees. Put the stuffing in a small roaster. Place the browned breasts over the stuffing. Pour any oil left in the pan over the ducks. Cover, and bake in the oven for 1 hour.

MAKES 2 TO 4 SERVINGS.

Bagged Duck or Goose

Bob Latendresse
Camden, Tennessee

2–4 ducks
1 (8-ounce) can crushed pineapple
1 (6-ounce) can frozen orange juice
Turkey-size oven bag

Preheat the oven to 350 degrees. Place the ducks in the oven bag and into a cooking pan. Pour the crushed pineapple and frozen orange juice over the ducks. Close the bag with its tie, and cut 4 to 6 small holes in the bag. Cook for 3 to 4 hours. You can cook a goose the same way, but cook for 4½ to 5 hours. You may quarter the goose.

SERVINGS WILL DEPEND ON AMOUNT OF DUCK OR GOOSE.

Hearty Duck and Bean Casserole

1 pound dried Great Northern beans
2 quarts water
4 duck breasts
¼ teaspoon ground cloves
2 bay leaves
1 large onion, chopped
1 pound mild or hot sausage
1 cup apple juice
1 (6-ounce) can tomato paste
1 teaspoon thyme
1 tablespoon parsley flakes

Put the beans in water, cover, and soak overnight; drain and combine with two quarts fresh water in a large saucepan. Add the rinsed duck breasts, cloves, and bay leaves to the beans. Bring to a boil, skim the foam, and simmer for one hour. Remove and slice the duck breasts. Cook the beans 15 minutes longer. Remove the bay leaves. Drain the beans, reserving the liquid. Cook the onion and sausage until crumbly; drain and add the apple juice, tomato paste, thyme, parsley flakes, duck, and two cups reserved bean liquid. Mix well and heat for 3 minutes. Preheat the oven to 375 degrees. Layer the bean mixture and sausage mixture alternately in a large casserole. Bake in the oven for 1 hour.

MAKES 6 TO 8 SERVINGS.

Duck Jambalaya

Sandy Pinkard

3	tablespoons bacon grease
3	tablespoons flour
2	medium onions, chopped
1	cup chopped green onions
2	tablespoons chopped fresh parsley
1	cup chopped celery
1	cup chopped green pepper
2	cloves garlic, minced
2	cups chicken stock
1	cup rice
2	teaspoons salt
$1/2$	teaspoon cayenne
4	cups duck meat for jambalaya (recipe follows)

In a large heavy pot, heat the bacon grease, and gradually add the flour, stirring constantly until the roux is dark brown. Add the onions, parsley, celery, green pepper, and garlic. Cook until soft. Add the chicken stock, a cup or so of water, rice, salt, cayenne, and duck meat. Bring to a boil; then lower heat as much as possible. Cook 1 hour, tightly covered. Stir occasionally. When the rice is done, remove the cover and cook a few more minutes so rice will steam dry.

MAKES 4 TO 6 SERVINGS.

Duck Meat for Jambalaya

2	large ducks
1	tablespoon salt
1	tablespoon pepper
1	onion, quartered
2	ribs celery
1	bay leaf

In a large pot, cook the ducks in water seasoned with salt, pepper, onion, celery, and bay leaf for about $1^{1}/_{2}$ hours, or until tender. Remove the ducks and cool. Remove the meat from the bone, and cut into bite-size pieces.

MAKES ABOUT 4 CUPS.

Crock-Pot Duck—Goose, Too

From a North Dakota Waterfowler

2	**ducks or 1 goose**
	Salt and pepper
	Garlic powder
	Salad oil
1	**($10^3/_4$-ounce) can condensed cream of mushroom soup**
1	**soup can of milk**
1	**onion, cut in chunks**
1	**(4-ounce) can mushrooms**

Cut up the bird(s), and soak for 8 hours in cold water in the refrigerator. Season the bird(s) with salt, pepper, and plenty of garlic powder. Brown the bird(s) in the oil. Place in a Crock-Pot with soup, milk, onion, and mushrooms. Cook for 6 to 8 hours.

MAKES 4 TO 6 SERVINGS.

To make a duck blind, cut a 3 x 3-foot piece of concrete reinforcement wire, and weave cane through the openings. Tie the cane in bundles with wire. The bottom edge should be cut leaving wire sticking down. When you get to the place where you want to hunt, simply poke the wire in the ground forming a "V" around you. This will also work in a dove field.

Four-Game Pot Pie

Salt and pepper

½ pound duck breast, skin removed

½ pound cubed venison

½ pound wild boar

½ pound rabbit loin

All-purpose flour for dusting

4 tablespoons vegetable oil

2 slices bacon

2 tablespoons butter

2 carrots, diced

1 celery rib, diced

10 mushrooms, diced

½ cup blanched pearl onions

4 tablespoons all-purpose flour

2 cups game stock or beef stock

1 bay leaf

2 tablespoons currant jelly

Pastry dough

1 egg, beaten with 1 tablespoon water

Salt and pepper the duck breast, cubed venison, wild boar, and rabbit loin. Dust with flour; then brown in a skillet over medium-high heat in oil. Remove meats from the skillet. Cut the bacon into 1-inch pieces and fry until crisp; remove from the pan. Melt the butter in the skillet, and add the carrots, celery, mushrooms, and blanched pearl onions. Sauté for 3 minutes and remove from the skillet. Lower the heat, stir in the flour, and cook for 2 minutes, stirring well. Raise the heat to medium, add the stock, bring to a boil, and then simmer for 2 minutes. Return the meats and vegetables to the skillet; add the bay leaf and currant jelly. Cover the pan, and simmer over low heat for 30 minutes. Preheat the oven to 400 degrees. Put the mixture in a large casserole dish, and top with pastry dough. Crimp the edges of the dough, brush the dough with the egg wash, and then cut several vents in the pastry to allow steam to escape. Place on a baking pan, and bake in the oven for 35 to 40 minutes, or until the crust is brown.

MAKES 5 TO 8 SERVINGS.

— GOOSE —

I've only eaten one goose. It was okay, but not as tasty as I thought it would be. It is generally better to pluck geese, as well as most other birds to be roasted. When skinned, some of the flavor is lost with the skin, and the meat may be dry (which I found to be true) when cooked.

Juicy Goosey

½ cup orange juice

½ cup dry white wine

¼ cup butter

1 tablespoon lemon juice

1 teaspoon basil

⅛ teaspoon orange rind

¼ teaspoon dry mustard

1 (4- to 5-pound) goose

Parsley sprigs

Orange wedges

Preheat the oven to 450 degrees. Heat the orange juice, wine, butter, lemon juice, basil, orange rind, and dry mustard in a small pan. Place the goose in a roasting pan, and pour a little of the hot orange sauce over the goose. Roast in the oven for 45 minutes, basting every 10 minutes with the sauce. Place the goose on a platter, and garnish with parsley sprigs and orange wedges. Carve the breast into thin slices and serve, ladling a little of the remaining sauce over the slices.

MAKES 4 TO 6 SERVINGS.

West Tennessee Goose

1 medium goose

4 to 5 quarts cold water

4 to 6 tablespoons salt

2 pounds lean beef

1 pound cracked beef bones

1 pound carrots, scraped

1 pound turnips, quartered

1 pound leeks, sliced

Garlic

Black pepper

Bay leaf

Thyme

1 cup white wine

French bread

Remove the skin of the goose, wash, and dry. Split the goose into halves. Using a large pot with a tight-fitting lid, pour in the water and dissolve the salt. Add the goose halves, the beef cut into squares, and the cracked beef bones. If the water doesn't cover all the meat, add enough water and more salt. Very slowly increase the temperature and remove the scum from the surface of the water as often as needed; the scum forms before liquid comes to a boil. Allow the mixture to boil, and add the carrots, turnips, leeks, and a little garlic. Season with the pepper, a bay leaf, and a pinch of thyme. Pour in the wine. Cover tightly, reduce heat to a bare simmer, and cook for 4 hours. Remove the goose, beef, and vegetables, and drain well; keep warm. Remove all the bones and bits of bones from the liquid in the pot. On large plates, place some of each vegetable on thick pieces of the French bread. Pour the liquid over all. Carve the goose, and serve with the beef.

MAKES 8 TO 12 SERVINGS.

— COOT —

Waterfowl hunters probably see more coots than they do any other species of ducks. Coots, or mud hens, are everywhere around waterfowl areas, and they don't fly off like most wild ducks do. They just sort of paddle around slowly, feeding on roots and so on.

Coots live on many of the same foods as other waterfowl, and they make an excellent dish when properly handled and prepared. All too often, people turn their noses up at coot, when in reality they are missing a most tasty wild fowl.

In fact, coots are easier to prepare than ducks, since they should always be skinned—the skin has a strong taste. After skinning, all fat must be removed. Then, before cooking, soak the coot for 4 to 6 hours in the refrigerator in a salt solution to which 2 tablespoons vinegar has been added.

Springville Bottoms Coot

Here's the best coot recipe I could come up with. It's been passed on from hunter to hunter at Springville Bottoms (West Sandy Wildlife Management Area) in Springville, Tennessee.
        —JIMMY

Skinned coot

Onions, cut to cover coot

Bacon fat

Salt and pepper

Clean the coot and cut off the head, feet, wings, and tail. Rinse the bird in cold water. Slice the coot into pieces, and slice the onions. Use a frying pan large enough to handle the coot and onions and stirring action without spilling over. Place the frying pan on low heat, and add a generous amount of bacon fat. When the fat is melted, add the onions to cover the bottom of the pan; then add the pieces of coot. Add salt and pepper to taste, and place a cover on the pan. Cook on low heat until done, stirring occasionally. If necessary, add a little water to prevent scorching.

MAKES 3 TO 4 SERVINGS.

Chapter 5

Big Feathered Game

Wild Turkey

Grilled Wild Turkey Strips

½ **cup (1 stick) melted butter**

3 **tablespoons lemon juice**

Salt and pepper

Wild turkey, cut in strips 1-inch thick

Warm the butter, and mix in the lemon juice and salt and pepper to taste. Baste the turkey strips, and place on a greased grill about 6 inches over hot coals. Grill for 5 or 6 minutes on each side, basting from time to time.

Beer-Can-in-a-Wild-Turkey (or Chicken)

I really like this. It's all I can do to keep my tongue from slapping me silly.

—JIMMY

1 **can beer**

Aluminum pie plate

Wild turkey or chicken

Oil

Salt and pepper

Paprika

Garlic

Herbs of choice

Wash a can of beer. Open the top, and punch holes in the top of the beer can. Pour one-third of the beer into a pie plate. Wash the turkey, and place it (or fryer chicken), rubbed with oil, in the pie plate. Put the salt, pepper, paprika, and garlic to taste in the beer can. Put the gizzard over the big hole in the beer can, and place the can inside the bird. Preheat the oven to 400 degrees, or prepare a hot grill. Cook the turkey or chicken for 1¼ hours.

SERVINGS WILL DEPEND ON THE SIZE OF THE TURKEY.

Broiled Wild Turkey Teriyaki

Lane Harms
Franklin, Tennessee

½ **cup soy sauce**

¼ **cup sake, dry vermouth, or sherry**

2 **tablespoons brown sugar**

1 **tablespoon finely grated fresh gingerroot**

2 **cloves finely grated garlic**
   Black pepper (optional)

1–2 **pounds wild turkey strips, cut 1-inch thick**
   Rice (cooked separately)
   Asian stir-fried vegetables (cooked separately)

Mix the soy sauce, sake, brown sugar, gingerroot, and garlic. Add the black pepper to taste (note that it is not a traditional teriyaki ingredient). Put the turkey strips into a non-metallic container, and pour the marinade over them. Stir the strips to coat all sides, and marinate in the refrigerator for 1 to 2 hours. Preheat the broiler. Broil the turkey strips for about 5 minutes on each side, basting two or three times with the leftover marinade. Test for doneness. Serve with rice and Asian stir-fried vegetables.

MAKES 4 TO 8 SERVINGS.

Honey-Baked Wild Turkey

Deloris Range
Oak Grove, Kentucky

6 **tablespoons honey**

1 **(10- to 12-pound) wild turkey**

1 **teaspoon salt**

1 **teaspoon coarse black pepper**
   Stuffing (see Chapter 9)

¾ **cup chopped onion**

2 **cups white wine**

½ **cup chicken broth**

1 **teaspoon parsley flakes**

1 **stick butter, melted**

1 **teaspoon Creole seasoning**

Preheat the oven to 325 degrees. Warm the honey, and brush the turkey with the honey; then sprinkle with salt and pepper. Place on a rack in a large baking pan. Place the stuffing inside the turkey. Mix the onion, wine, broth, and parsley, and then add the butter and Creole seasoning. Baste the bird with the wine mixture. Place in the oven, and roast for 4 hours, basting occasionally with the wine mixture.

MAKES 10 TO 15 SERVINGS.

Cajun Fried Wild Turkey

Lane Harms
Franklin, Tennessee

1   **(12- to 18-pound) wild turkey with skin**

5   **ounces A.1. steak sauce**

5   **ounces Tiger Sauce**

5   **ounces Heinz 57 Sauce**

2   **cups barbecue sauce**

3   **ounces liquid smoke**

½   **cup Tony Chachere's Creole Seasoning**

5   **gallons peanut oil for frying**

If frozen, thaw the turkey completely. Mix the A.1., Tiger, Heinz 57, and barbecue sauces with the liquid smoke and Tony's seasoning; simmer for 30 minutes. Place the warm mixture in a large hypodermic syringe, and inject the bird about every square inch all the way to the bone. Push in the mixture as you slowly remove the syringe. Refrigerate overnight. Heat the cooking oil to 350 degrees (you must maintain this temperature). Place the turkey in a frying basket, and lower it into the oil. Make sure the oil completely covers the turkey. Deep-fry for 3 to 4 minutes per pound.

MAKES 12 OR MORE SERVINGS.

During the late season, gobblers spend lots of time strutting in areas where they've picked up hens in the past. Find one of these spots, set up, and wait, calling only occasionally with soft clucks and purrs. It may take a few hours, but odds are good a tom will come in, often without making a sound. Be ready.

Wild Turkey Casserole

Mrs. Ethel Wells
Nashville, Tennessee

3   tablespoons olive oil

2   large carrots, peeled and diced

3   celery ribs, thinly sliced

1   medium onion, minced

5   garlic cloves, minced

3   (15-ounce) cans drained white kidney beans or Great Northern beans

1   (6-ounce) can tomato sauce

2 to 3 cups cooked wild turkey, cut in 1½-inch pieces

¾   pound smoked turkey sausage, cut in ½-inch thick slices

1½ cups canned or homemade chicken or turkey broth

½   teaspoon dried thyme leaves

    Pinch of ground cloves

    Salt and pepper

1   cup coarse white bread crumbs

½   cup fresh minced parsley

Preheat the oven to 350 degrees. Heat 1½ tablespoons of the olive oil over medium-high heat in a Dutch oven or ovenproof casserole dish. Add the carrots, celery, onion, and 3 of the minced garlic cloves. Sauté until softened, 5 to 7 minutes. Remove from the heat, and add the beans, tomato sauce, turkey, and smoked sausage. Pour in the broth, and stir to combine all the ingredients thoroughly. Season with thyme, cloves, salt, and pepper. Cover the Dutch oven or casserole, and bake in the oven for 45 minutes. Mix bread crumbs, parsley, the remaining garlic, and the remaining 1½ tablespoons olive oil. Uncover the casserole, and sprinkle the crumb mixture over the top. Continue baking, uncovered, until the crumbs are lightly browned and the casserole is bubbling, about 20 minutes more.

MAKES 6 TO 8 SERVINGS.

Wild Turkey Fried Rice

3   tablespoons light brown
     sugar
1   teaspoon peeled and minced
     fresh ginger
1/4 teaspoon crushed red pepper
1/2 cup rice vinegar
3   tablespoons low-salt soy
     sauce
2   tablespoons water
1   tablespoon crunchy peanut
     butter
2   teaspoons vegetable oil
1   pound 1/4-inch-thick wild
     turkey breast cutlets, cut
     into 1-inch chunks
2   garlic cloves, minced
4   cups cooked rice
1/4 cup chopped green onions
3   tablespoons chopped,
     unsalted, dry-roasted
     peanuts
     Sliced green onions
     (optional)

Combine the sugar, ginger, red pepper, rice vinegar, soy sauce, water, and peanut butter in a bowl. Stir with a whisk until blended. Heat the oil in a large, nonstick skillet over medium-high heat. Add the turkey and garlic, and stir-fry for 3 minutes, or until the turkey is done. Add the rice, and stir-fry for 2 minutes. Remove the mixture from the skillet and keep warm. Add the vinegar mixture to the skillet and stir-fry for 1 minute. Remove from the heat. Stir in the chopped green onions and peanuts. Garnish with sliced green onions, if desired.

MAKES 6 SERVINGS.

Rub Armor-All into the Jake decoy to make it shine like a real turkey. Incoming gobblers will accept it more readily when it appears more lifelike.

If you hunt wild turkeys, search out water holes and streams during hot, dry weather. Unless the woods are wet, turkeys will go to water every day and leave signs such as feathers, droppings, and tracks. Set up a blind or hunker back against a wide tree, and wait patiently. Call lightly occasionally, or simply wait the birds out.

Wild Turkey Leftovers

John and Denise Phillips

Here's the answer to the question, "What do I do with the leftovers?"
—DENISE PHILLIPS

2 cups chopped, cooked wild turkey

½ cup chopped almonds

2 cups chopped celery

⅓ cup chopped green bell pepper

2 tablespoons chopped pimiento

1 cup shredded Swiss or cheddar cheese

½ cup mayonnaise

2 tablespoons lemon juice

1 teaspoon salt

¼ teaspoon black pepper

1 cup crushed potato chips

Combine the turkey, almonds, celery, bell pepper, pimiento, cheese, mayonnaise, lemon juice, salt, and pepper. Preheat the oven to 350 degrees. Pour the mixture into a greased 2-quart casserole. Bake in the oven for 30 minutes. Remove from the oven, and sprinkle potato chips on top of the turkey mixture. Return to the oven, and bake until chips are lightly browned, about 10 minutes.

MAKES 4 TO 6 SERVINGS.

Four Wild Turkey Togas

Mrs. Warren Maddux

1 cup creamy Caesar dressing

4 (12-inch) flour tortillas

12 leaves romaine lettuce

2 cups cooked chopped wild turkey

1 (7-ounce) jar drained roasted red peppers

¼ cup grated Parmesan cheese

Spread 2 to 3 tablespoons of Caesar dressing over the surface of each tortilla. Place 3 lettuce leaves on each tortilla, and press them into the dressing. Place the turkey and roasted red peppers equally on one half of each tortilla. Sprinkle the Parmesan cheese over the top, and roll each tightly, starting with the turkey side. Wrap individually, and refrigerate for 1 hour. Cut each wrap to size before serving.

MAKES 4 SERVINGS.

Chapter 6

Small Hairy Critters

Rabbit, Squirrel, Raccoon, Groundhog, Opossum,
Woodchuck, Muskrat, Beaver

⌐ RABBIT ⌐

Rabbit My Way—Cove Hollow Style

Dean Buck
Silver Point, Tennessee

2	**(10¾-ounce) cans condensed cream of mushroom soup**
1	**soup can water**
⅔	**cup tomato juice**
1	**diced onion**
¼	**cup dried or fresh parsley**
1	**teaspoon salt**
1	**teaspoon pepper**
	Soy sauce or Worcestershire sauce (optional, use less salt)
2	**rabbits, cut in pieces**

Preheat the oven to 150 to 180 degrees. In a large bowl, mix the mushroom soup, water, tomato juice, onion, parsley, salt, pepper, and soy or Worcestershire sauce. When completely blended, pour ½ inch of the mixture in a large baking pan. Add the rabbits and the rest of the mixture. Cover and bake in the oven for 2 hours.

MAKES 6 TO 8 SERVINGS.

Grilled Barbecued Rabbit

C. K. Wright
Nashville, Tennessee

2 rabbits

Salt and pepper

¼ cup butter

¼ cup lard

½ cup lemon juice

Barbecue sauce
(recipe follows)

Parboil the rabbits in water, salt, and pepper in a covered vessel until the thick parts are tender to the touch of a fork. Remove from the pan, and cook over a charcoal fire for 30 to 45 minutes. In a small saucepan on the stovetop, melt the butter and lard, and add the lemon juice. While cooking the rabbits, baste often with the lemon-butter mixture. During the last 15 minutes of grilling, baste the rabbits frequently with the barbecue sauce.

MAKES 4 TO 8 SERVINGS.

Barbecue Sauce

1 medium onion,
chopped fine

2 tablespoons butter

2 tablespoons vinegar

2 tablespoons brown sugar

4 tablespoons lemon juice

1 cup catsup

3 tablespoons Worcestershire
sauce

½ tablespoon prepared
mustard

½ cup water

Salt

Brown the onions and butter in a saucepan. Mix, when browned, with the vinegar, brown sugar, lemon juice, catsup, Worcestershire sauce, mustard, water, and salt to taste. Allow to simmer 30 minutes over low heat.

MAKES 3 TO 4 CUPS.

If you suspect a rabbit is in some cover ahead of you, walk steadily toward it and be ready to fire when you stop. Rabbits usually flush when you stop walking.

Baked Rabbit

Pauline Wells
Camden, Tennessee

1   rabbit, cut into serving
      pieces
      Melted margarine
      Finely crushed Ritz crackers

Preheat the oven to 300 degrees. Dip the rabbit pieces in melted margarine, and roll in the crushed Ritz crackers. Bake at 300 degrees until tender.

MAKES 2 TO 4 SERVINGS.

Spicy Baked Barbecued Rabbit

Louise Murphy
Ashland City, Tennessee

1   cup tomato catsup
½   cup Worcestershire sauce
1   tablespoon vinegar
3   tablespoons lemon juice
        Salt
1   teaspoon cayenne
1   rabbit

Preheat the oven to 350 degrees. Mix the catsup, Worcestershire sauce, vinegar, lemon juice, salt, and red pepper to make the barbecue sauce. Bake the rabbit in the oven in a pan with a little water for 45 minutes, or until tender. Pour the barbecue sauce over the rabbit, and continue baking for another hour, basting often.

MAKES 2 TO 4 SERVINGS.

German-Style Rabbit

Maureen Irons
Charlotte, Tennessee

1   **rabbit**
¼   **pound bacon**
     Salt and pepper
2   **tablespoons butter**
2   **tablespoons potato flour**
1   **pint sour cream**
1   **teaspoon salt**
     Dash of pepper

Singe the rabbit after it has been carefully cleaned, wash it in several cold water rinses, and cut it into 5 pieces. Fry the bacon in an ovenproof skillet until the fat is fried out. Add the rabbit to the skillet, cook until brown, and then dust with salt and pepper. Preheat the oven to 350 degrees. Cover the skillet, and bake the rabbit in the oven for about 1 hour. Remove the rabbit from the pan and place on a dish. Add the butter to the pan, and stir until the butter browns; then add the potato flour. Mix well and add the sour cream. Stir until boiling. Add a teaspoon salt and a dash of pepper, and pour the sauce over the rabbit.

MAKES 2 TO 4 SERVINGS.

Rabbit Smothered in Onions

Faye Anderton
Tullahoma, Tennessee

1   **(3-pound) rabbit, cut in**
     serving pieces
     All-purpose flour
3   **large onions, sliced**
3   **tablespoons shortening**
1   **cup sour cream**
     Salt and pepper

Dredge the rabbit pieces in the flour. Sauté the onions in the shortening in a skillet, remove the onions from the skillet, and sauté the rabbit in the remaining shortening until brown on all sides. Cover the rabbit with the onions, and pour the sour cream over the top of the rabbit and onions. Cover and cook slowly for 1 hour on top of the stove. Alternatively, cover and bake in a 350-degree oven for 35 to 45 minutes; uncover and bake 15 minutes longer. Season with salt and pepper.

MAKES 2 TO 4 SERVINGS.

 Don't walk in a straight line toward a rabbit or even look directly toward it. Walk slowly toward the wind, and pick up something from the ground to study to throw the rabbit off-guard.

Fried Rabbit

Anonymous
Lebanon, Tennessee

Ninety percent of the rabbit hunters that I hunt with and talk with tell me you can't beat frying rabbit just like you do chicken. Clean your rabbits well and soak them overnight in salt water in the refrigerator. Cut rabbit pieces as you like, and sprinkle well with flour. Some guys and gals use an egg/milk batter, and then they flour the rabbit pieces. I guess it just depends on how you like the crust on fried rabbit or chicken. Cook slowly on medium heat. You can make some mighty tasty gravy from the drippings.

—ANONYMOUS HUNTER

1 **rabbit, cut to serving sizes**

All-purpose flour

Salt and pepper

Oil for frying

Dredge the rabbit pieces in flour, salt, and pepper. Cook in the oil on medium heat until done.

MAKES 2 TO 4 SERVINGS.

Beer Hasenpfeffer

Chapel Hill Rabbit Hunters
Chapel Hill, Tennessee

1   cup vinegar

1   (12-ounce) can beer

2   large onions, sliced

1   tablespoon mixed
    pickling spices

1   teaspoon salt

1/8 teaspoon pepper

1   large rabbit, cut in
    serving portions

1/4 cup all-purpose flour

1/2 cup fat

1   tablespoon sugar

Combine the vinegar, beer, onions, pickling spices, salt, and pepper in a large earthenware bowl. Add the meat, cover, and let stand in a refrigerator 1 to 2 days, turning the meat several times during that period. Dry the meat with a cloth or absorbent paper, and dip it in the flour. Melt the fat in a large skillet, and brown the meat on all sides. Pour off the fat. Strain the marinade, and add it to the meat in the skillet along with the sugar. Bring the mixture to a boil. Reduce the heat, cover, and simmer for 40 minutes, or until the meat is tender. Thicken the liquid with flour mixed with water, if desired. Serve with potato dumplings, buttered green beans, and a green salad.

MAKES 2 TO 3 SERVINGS.

Stewed Rabbit

2   rabbits

    Salt and pepper

2   medium onions, finely
    chopped

3   tablespoons vegetable oil

1   ham, cut into 1-inch cubes

1   cup water

1   (8-ounce) can mushrooms

2   tablespoons sherry

Clean the rabbits, and cut at the joints into serving pieces. Rub each piece with salt and pepper. Brown the rabbit and onions in vegetable oil; then add the cubed ham, water, mushrooms, and sherry. Stir well, and adjust seasoning to taste. Simmer 1 hour.

MAKES 6 TO 8 SERVINGS.

Rabbit Meat Loaf

Christyne Wolfe
Lascassas, Tennessee

1½ pounds ground rabbit meat

1 large or 2 small eggs

1 cup cracker crumbs or bread crumbs

Poultry seasoning

1 tablespoon chopped celery

1 tablespoon chopped green pepper

Preheat the oven to 350 degrees. Combine the rabbit, egg, cracker crumbs or bread crumbs, poultry seasoning to taste, celery, and green pepper. Form the mixture into a loaf. Place it in a greased loaf pan, and bake in the oven approximately 1 hour and 15 minutes or until done.

MAKES 8 TO 10 SERVINGS.

— SQUIRREL —

Squirrel and Dumplings

2 squirrels, cut into serving pieces

1 onion, chopped

1 bay leaf

Salt and pepper

1 large can biscuit dough

Place the squirrels, onion, bay leaf, salt, and pepper into a stew pan with water, and cook until the meat is tender. Roll the biscuit dough out very thin. For dumplings, cut strips 1 inch wide and 4 inches long. Add these to the stew pot, and cook until dumplings are firm. Serve hot.

MAKES 4 TO 6 SERVINGS.

The great thing about hunting squirrels with a bow and arrow is that the squirrel is comparable to the modern-day big game animals in the way they react to hunting pressure. Like deer, the more pressure put on squirrels, the older and wiser they become. Squirrels under hunting pressure will provide the bow hunter with some very challenging sessions.

Southern Fried Squirrel

Pearl Scarbrough
Murfreesboro, Tennessee

I've had this recipe for 30 years or more. —PEARL SCARBROUGH

2	squirrels, disjointed to serving size
1	onion
1	carrot
1	stalk celery
1	sprig parsley
	Batter (recipe follows)

Drop the squirrel pieces slowly into boiling water to cover. Cut up the onion, carrot, celery, and parsley. Add to the pot, and simmer until tender. Cool thoroughly. Dry the squirrel pieces between paper towels. Prepare the batter. Dip each piece of squirrel into the batter; then drop into deep hot fat, and fry until pieces are golden brown.

MAKES 1 TO 2 SERVINGS.

Batter

½	cup flour
½	cup cornmeal
1	teaspoon baking powder
¼	teaspoon salt
1	egg, beaten
¼	cup milk

Mix the flour, cornmeal, baking powder, and salt. Beat the egg lightly. Add the milk, and stir liquid mixture into the dry ingredients.

Squirrel Pot Pie

Sharon Benefield
Kingston, Tennessee

I thought you might like this down-home recipe that was used by my ancestors. It is tried and true.
—SHARON BENEFIELD

3 squirrels

½ cup all-purpose flour

3 tablespoons butter

1 quart boiling water

1 onion, chopped

1 teaspoon salt

¼ teaspoon pepper

Biscuits from a 10-biscuit can

Lemon juice (optional)

Sherry (optional)

Worcestershire sauce (optional)

Cut the squirrels into serving pieces, and roll them in flour. Melt 2 tablespoons of the butter in a saucepan. Sauté the squirrels until brown. Add the boiling water, onion, salt, and pepper; cover and simmer 1 hour. Lay biscuit rounds on the squirrel to make a crust. Cover, and boil gently for 15 minutes. Remove the crusts and squirrels to a hot platter. Melt the remaining tablespoon of butter, and add to the liquid in the pan, mixing well. Pour the mixture over the squirrels and crust. If desired, lemon juice, sherry, or Worcestershire sauce may be added to the gravy before serving.

MAKES 6 TO 8 SERVINGS.

Squirrels like corn. Locating a cornfield next to a wooded area should increase your odds of seeing gray and fox squirrels.

— RACCOON —

Baked Raccoon with Apples

1   medium raccoon

     Stuffing (recipe follows)

4   strips salt pork

4   large onions

2   cups beef stock

Skin and clean the raccoon. Wash well, and remove most of the fat. Place in a large soup kettle, cover with water, and bring to a boil. Lower the heat and simmer for 30 minutes. Make the stuffing. Take the raccoon out of the cooking juices and cool. Preheat the oven to 400 degrees. Stuff the raccoon, and sew up the cavity. Place the raccoon breast down on the rack of a roasting pan, with the legs folded under the body and fastened with a string. Drape the salt pork over the back of the raccoon, and fasten with toothpicks. Place the onions beside the raccoon on the rack. Bake at 400 degrees for 10 minutes to brown the meat, and then reduce the heat to 325 degrees. Add the beef stock. Cook for 1 hour, basting as often as possible. Transfer to a heated platter, and surround with the onions.

SERVINGS WILL DEPEND ON THE SIZE OF THE RACCOON.

Stuffing

5   large tart apples

2   tablespoons butter, melted

1   teaspoon cinnamon

1   cup dry bread crumbs

1   teaspoon salt

½   teaspoon pepper

Peel, core, and dice the apples; put in a mixing bowl. Add the butter, cinnamon, bread crumbs, salt, and pepper to the apples. Mix well.

Stuffed Roast Raccoon

1   **pound sweet potatoes, cooked and mashed**

½   **cup raisins**

1   **cup bread crumbs**

2   **apples, peeled and chopped**

¼   **cup butter, melted**

    Salt and pepper

4 to 5 pound raccoon

First make the stuffing by mixing sweet potatoes, raisins, bread crumbs, apples, butter, salt, and pepper. Preheat the oven to 325 degrees. Wash the raccoon meat thoroughly and dry with a cloth. Cut off some of the fat, leaving just enough for a thin layer. Salt the inside of the raccoon, and stuff gently with the sweet potato mixture. Sew the opening shut. Bake for 3 to 4 hours. When half done, turn the raccoon over so all the sides will be browned.

MAKES 6 TO 8 SERVINGS.

Keeping fish or game on ice maintains freshness. Freeze water in plastic bottles to put in your ice chest. It thaws more slowly than ice cubes. You also have drinking water as it thaws.

— GROUNDHOG —

Groundhog in Sour Cream

1   groundhog

½   cup vinegar

1   tablespoon salt

2   quarts water plus ½ cup

2   teaspoons baking soda

½   cup all-purpose flour

1   teaspoon salt

½   teaspoon allspice

½   cup bacon fat

3   wild onions or green onions, sliced

1   cup sour cream

Skin and clean the groundhog. Wash, dry, and put in an earthen crock. Cover with water, add vinegar and salt, and let stand in the refrigerator overnight. The next morning, remove from the brine, wash, and pat dry. In a large soup kettle, combine the 2 quarts water with the baking soda, and bring to a boil. Lower the heat, and simmer for 15 minutes, removing the scum as it rises. Drain and rinse the ground hog meat, and cut into serving pieces. Combine the flour, salt, and allspice, and dredge the pieces of meat in the mixture. Preheat the oven to 325 degrees. Cook the bacon grease in a heavy iron frying pan until smoking. Brown the meat on all sides, and transfer it to a greased four-quart casserole. Arrange the sliced onions on top; add the ½ cup water, cover, and bake for two hours, or until the meat is tender. Transfer the meat to a heated platter to keep warm. Put the casserole on top of the stove over medium heat. Heat and spoon in the sour cream, stirring constantly. Do not let the sauce come to a boil. Put the meat back into the casserole, and simmer for about 15 minutes. Serve with creamed dandelion greens.

SERVINGS WILL DEPEND ON THE SIZE OF THE GROUNDHOG.

— OPOSSUM —

Opossum Roast

1   opossum
    Salt and pepper
1   onion, chopped
1   tablespoon fat
1   opossum liver
1   cup bread crumbs
¼   teaspoon Worcestershire
    sauce
1   hard-cooked egg
1   teaspoon salt
6   strips bacon, uncooked
1   quart water

Rub the opossum with salt and pepper. Brown the onion in the fat. Add the opossum liver, and cook until tender. Add bread crumbs, Worcestershire sauce, egg, salt, and just enough water to make a moist stuffing. Mix thoroughly, and stuff the opossum's cavity. Truss like a fowl. Preheat the oven to 350 degrees. Put the stuffed opossum in a roasting pan with bacon across its back, and pour the 1 quart water into the pan. Roast uncovered until tender, about 2 hours and 30 minutes. Baste every 15 minutes. Serve with sweet potatoes.

MAKES 2 TO 4 SERVINGS.

Fried Opossum

1   opossum
    Marinade (prepared
    or see Chapter 8)
1   cup flour
⅛   teaspoon paprika
    Dash of pepper
    Dash of tarragon
    Dash of thyme
    Oil

Soak the opossum for 2 hours in the refrigerator, in salt water, 1 quart water to 4 tablespoons salt. Rinse and dry the meat well. Cut the meat into frying-size chunks, and marinate it in the refrigerator for 7 hours. Coat each piece with a mixture of flour, paprika, pepper, tarragon, and thyme. Fry chunks of prepared opossum in oil until golden brown.

MAKES 2 TO 4 SERVINGS.

— WOODCHUCK —

Woodchuck Stew

1 **woodchuck**

Vinegar

2 **onions, sliced**

Salt

½ **cup sliced celery**

Cloves

Salt and pepper

All-purpose flour

Clean the woodchuck, remove its glands, and cut into serving pieces. Soak overnight in the refrigerator in a solution of equal parts of water and vinegar with the addition of 1 onion, sliced, and a little salt. Drain, wash, and wipe dry. Parboil the woodchuck for 20 minutes, drain, and cover with fresh boiling water. Add the remaining sliced onion, the celery, a few cloves, salt, and pepper to taste. Cook until tender. Thicken the gravy with the flour.

SERVINGS WILL DEPEND ON THE SIZE OF THE WOODCHUCK.

— MUSKRAT —

Smothered Muskrat and Onions

1 **muskrat, dressed and disjointed**

Salted water

1½ **teaspoons salt**

¼ **teaspoon paprika**

½ **cup flour**

3 **tablespoons fat**

3 **large onions**

1 **cup sour cream**

Soak the muskrat overnight in the salted water (1 tablespoon salt to 1 quart water) in the refrigerator. Remove from salted water, and season with 1 teaspoon of the salt, and the paprika; roll in the flour, and fry in fat until browned. Cover the muskrat with the onions, sprinkling onions with the remaining ½ teaspoon salt. Pour in the sour cream. Cover the skillet tightly, and simmer for 1 hour.

MAKES 4 SERVINGS.

Muskrat Meat Loaf

1½ **pounds ground muskrat**

¼ **teaspoon thyme**

1 **teaspoon salt**

2 **eggs, beaten**

1 **teaspoon Worcestershire sauce**

⅓ **cup bread crumbs**

¼ **teaspoon pepper**

1 **cup evaporated milk**

¼ **cup minced or grated onion**

Soak the muskrat overnight in salted water (1 tablespoon salt to 1 quart water) in the refrigerator. Drain, remove the meat from the bones, and grind. Mix the ground meat thoroughly with the thyme, salt, eggs, Worcestershire sauce, bread crumbs, pepper, evaporated milk, and onion. Preheat the oven to 350 degrees. Put the meat mixture in a meat loaf dish, and place the dish in a pan containing about 1 inch of hot water. Bake in the oven for 1½ to 2 hours.

MAKES 6 TO 8 SERVINGS.

— BEAVER —

Beaver Tail

1 **beaver tail**

Salt and pepper

Hold the beaver tail over an open flame until rough skin blisters. Remove from heat. When cool, peel off the skin. Roast the tail over coals, or simmer until tender; add salt and pepper to taste.

SERVINGS WILL DEPEND ON THE SIZE OF THE BEAVER TAIL.

Beaver or Raccoon Roast with Barbecue Sauce

1   small to medium beaver or raccoon, cut into serving-size pieces

½   teaspoon salt

1   teaspoon instant minced onion

3   tablespoons brown sugar

½   cup chili sauce

1½ teaspoons Worcestershire sauce

7   ounces beer or pickle juice

Preheat the oven to 350 degrees. Place the pieces of beaver or raccoon in a foil-lined roasting pan, and roast, covered, for 30 minutes. Meanwhile, mix salt, onion, brown sugar, chili sauce, Worcestershire sauce, and beer or pickle juice in a small bowl to make barbecue sauce. After the meat has cooked for 30 minutes, uncover and pour barbecue sauce over the pieces. Then roast, uncovered, for another 30 minutes to 1 hour, or until tender. During the cooking, baste several times with the barbecue sauce.

MAKES 4 TO 6 SERVINGS.

Fried Beaver

1   small beaver, cleaned and skinned

6   slices bacon

1   teaspoon seasoning salt

Remove the fat from the beaver, cut into serving pieces (strips or cubes), and soak overnight in cold water in the refrigerator. Drain. Cook in small amount of water until tender, and then fry with the bacon and seasoning salt.

MAKES 4 SERVINGS.

Variation:

Substitute hickory-smoked seasoning salt for plain seasoning salt.

Chapter 7

Big Hairy Critters

Venison, Antelope, Bear, Boar

— VENISON —

GETTING RID OF THE WILD TASTE

The most important step in preparing any kind of wild game or fish is washing it thoroughly. Venison, for instance, must be washed, washed, and then washed again to get blood out of the meat. You'll never remove all of it, but try. If the meat isn't cleaned properly, then it will have that wild taste that so many people don't care for.

I've had many ladies tell me that their husbands bring home deer meat, but they don't like it because of its wild taste. I've tasted cooked venison with that wild taste, and I agree.

Gary Modisett, a friend of mine, does some really great cooking and has shown me numerous ways to prepare venison. Gary sells seasoning packets that were prepared especially to take the wild taste out of wild game.

"I started working on recipes to cook venison and other wild game meat because all I heard from many hunters' wives was they didn't like it because of its wild taste," he said.

Gary's venison chili seasoning is terrific. His char-steak and fajita seasonings are just what the doctor ordered to rid wild game meats of their wild taste. [To order the seasoning packets, contact Gary Modisett, 3324 Freeman Hollow, Goodlettsville, TN 37072, (615) 859-1851.]

PREPARING VENISON

If you are like many hunters, once you have harvested a big game animal, you feel that the main object of the hunt has been accomplished. However, now is the time to think about the rewards of eating the game you've harvested.

Preparing your trophy deer for eating requires that the game be bled at once. Failure to do this immediately will impair the quality of the meat. You will need to insert a sharp knife at the base of the neck where it joins the chest (brisket), and cut the artery at that point.

Keep the wound open and free of clotting blood. The more blood drained off, the better.

Your deer will now need to be field dressed as quickly as possible. This requires a very sharp knife and also a sturdy blade. Take your time. You'll find satisfaction in doing a good job.

The field dressing chore is simple enough and need not be a messy one, unless the deer is badly shot up—another good argument for accurate shooting. It will save you trouble and waste less meat.

Carelessness, delay in dressing out, or failure to cool the deer meat completely and quickly are problems to avoid. The carcass should hang in a cool place with one or two sticks cut to the right length inserted between the walls of the body cavity to permit free circulation of air. Deer hide is an excellent insulating layer, and unless cool air can flow freely to the open flesh, the cooling may take many hours.

Don't be bashful while you're carrying or dragging your deer back to your vehicle or hunting camp. Tennessee's deer population has grown by leaps and bounds, and there are literally thousands of hunters that roam the hills and hollows in search of big bucks. For safety's sake, whistle, sing, or create some sort of human noise, and tie a piece of red cloth on the antlers so that other hunters will be sure to see or hear you.

Jimmy's Onion-Roasted Venison

1 (4-pound) rump or shoulder roast

Cooking fat

Salt and pepper

1 package dry onion soup mix

½ cup water

Preheat the oven to 300 degrees. In a large iron skillet, brown the roast in the cooking fat on all sides on top of the stove. Season with salt and pepper to taste. Sprinkle the package of onion soup mix on and around the roast. Add the water. Put the roast in a covered pan and bake in the oven for 2½ to 3 hours, until tender.

MAKES 6 TO 12 SERVINGS.

Venison Roast with Mushrooms

Mrs. Clayton Owens
Palmyra, Tennessee

4	tablespoons shortening
3	pounds boned and rolled venison roast
1	large onion, sliced
1	cup water
1	cup tomato juice
1	teaspoon salt
1	teaspoon black pepper
1	teaspoon sugar
1	bay leaf
2	bouillon cubes
4	(3-ounce) cans sliced mushrooms
½	cup red wine

Heat the shortening in a roasting pan on top of the stove. Add the roast, brown on all sides, add the onion, and brown 5 minutes longer. Combine the water, tomato juice, salt, pepper, and sugar, and pour over the meat. Remove from the heat. Add the bay leaf, bouillon cubes, and mushrooms; cover. Bake at 325 degrees for about 2 hours and 15 minutes. Add the wine and bake for 15 minutes longer.

MAKES 6 TO 8 SERVINGS.

Venison Shoulder Roast the Easy Way

1	medium venison shoulder roast
	Worcestershire sauce
	Lemon juice
6	strips bacon or fat back
1	stick butter
1	large onion, chopped
6	carrots, chopped
1	(10¾-ounce) can condensed cream of mushroom soup
1	soup can water

Preheat the oven to 300 degrees. Place the clean, well-trimmed venison shoulder in a large Dutch oven, and sprinkle with the Worcestershire sauce and lemon juice. Cover with the bacon strips, pats of butter, onion, and carrots. Add the soup and the water. Place in the oven and bake for 4 hours, basting occasionally and adding water as needed to keep moist. Serve with potatoes or rice pilaf.

MAKES 4 TO 6 SERVINGS.

Venison Pot Roast

Christyne Wolfe
Lascassas, Tennessee

3–5 pounds venison roast

2 teaspoons salt

½ teaspoon black pepper

½ cup all-purpose flour

3 tablespoons fat

4–6 small onions

1 cup water

Potatoes (optional)

Carrots (optional)

Season the venison with salt and pepper, and dredge in the flour. In a large Dutch oven, brown the venison on all sides in hot fat, adding the onions and water. Cover and simmer until tender, 2 to 3 hours. Potatoes and carrots may be added 20 to 30 minutes before the roast is done.

MAKES 6 TO 10 SERVINGS.

Venison Pot Roast with Vegetables and Sour Cream

Haunch or loin of venison

Lard

Salt pork

3 medium onions, sliced

4 carrots, chopped

2 small turnips, chopped

4 ribs celery, chopped

Finely chopped parsley

Pinch of rosemary

Pinch of thyme

2 strips lemon peel

8 peppercorns

2 bay leaves

Salt

Dry red wine

½ cup sour cream

Trim carefully, and remove all surplus fibers, skin, and fat from the venison haunch or loin. In a large skillet, brown the venison in the lard with the salt pork. Place the onions, carrots, turnips, celery, parsley, rosemary, thyme, lemon peel, peppercorns, bay leaves, and salt in a Dutch oven with equal parts of red wine and water, a total of 3 to 4 cups liquid. Bring the mixture to a boil, and let simmer for 30 minutes. Add the larded venison and cover. Simmer for 2 hours. Remove the meat, strain the sauce, and place the venison in a roasting pan. Pour the strained sauce over the roast, adding sour cream, and cook slowly until well done.

MAKES 4 TO 8 SERVINGS.

Barbecued Venison Roast

Andy and Betty Thomason
Columbia, Tennessee

When you prepare your venison for the freezer, be sure to cut two or three large roasts for this delicious barbecue. —BETTY THOMASON

1   **venison roast**

    Salt and pepper

    All-purpose flour

    Shortening

    Barbecue sauce (recipe follows)

Rinse the venison roast in cool water. Sprinkle the roast with salt and pepper. Roll in the flour, and brown in 2 tablespoons of shortening in a large iron skillet. Turn the roast to brown on all sides. Put the roast in a large pot with a lid, and cook on top of the stove until tender. Remove from the pot and let cool. Remove any excess fat and bone. Chop the meat. Add the barbecue sauce to the chopped meat, and let simmer for 30 to 40 minutes. (This recipe also freezes well.)

SERVINGS WILL DEPEND ON THE SIZE OF THE ROAST.

Note:

If you are in a hurry, you may follow the recipe using your favorite pre-made barbecue sauce.

Barbecue Sauce

½   **cup vinegar**

9   **ounces Heinz chili sauce**

1   **medium onion, chopped**

2   **tablespoons sugar**

    One red pepper pod

Mix the vinegar, chili sauce, onion, sugar, and red pepper.

Venison Neck Roast with Gravy

Salt and pepper

Venison neck

1 (10 ¾-ounce) can condensed golden mushroom soup

Rice

Preheat the oven to 350 degrees. Salt and pepper the deer neck heavily; repeat. Wrap the neck in several layers of aluminum foil. Place in a pan in the oven for 30 to 45 minutes. Turn the oven to 250 degrees, and leave for 4 to 6 hours. Remove from the oven and unwrap, saving all liquids. Remove the meat from the bones (it will fall off). Cut meat against the grain into bite-size pieces. Mix the drippings with 1 can of golden mushroom soup, and then pour over the meat. Add water to give gravy consistency. Cook rice according to package directions. Reheat meat and gravy and serve over rice.

MAKES 4 TO 5 SERVINGS.

Fried Venison Backstrap

Fred Scarbrough
Murfreesboro, Tennessee

2 cups bread crumbs or crushed Ritz crackers

1½ teaspoons parsley flakes

Salt and pepper

2 pounds venison backstrap

1 egg, beaten

Mix the crumbled bread or cracker crumbs, parsley, and salt and pepper to taste. Dip the pieces of backstrap into the egg and then into bread crumbs. Cover and fry for 25 minutes.

MAKES 6 TO 8 SERVINGS.

Grilled Venison Steaks

William & Andrea Bolden
Unionville, Tennessee

8   venison steaks
1   (10-ounce) bottle Worcestershire sauce
1   (6-ounce) bottle A.1. steak sauce
¹/₃ cup lemon pepper
    Garlic salt
1 ¹/₂ onions, minced

Marinate the steaks overnight in the refrigerator in a mixture of Worcestershire sauce, A.1. sauce, lemon pepper, garlic salt, and onions, turning occasionally. Put the steaks on the grill, and baste with the remaining marinade until desired doneness.

MAKES 8 SERVINGS.

Fried Venison Steaks

Mildred Curle
Nashville, Tennessee

    Venison steaks
¹/₂ cup vinegar
1   egg, beaten
    Salt and pepper
    Garlic salt
    Cracker crumbs
    All-purpose flour
    Cooking oil

Marinate the steaks in the refrigerator in the vinegar with just enough water to cover for at least 1 hour. Remove steaks from the marinade, and dip into the egg. Sprinkle with the salt and pepper to taste and the garlic salt, and roll in cracker crumbs with a little flour added. Fry in a moderate amount of cooking oil until golden brown.

SERVINGS WILL DEPEND ON THE NUMBER OF STEAKS.

Venison Steak and Gravy

William and Andrea Bolden
Unionville, Tennessee

Venison steak

Salted water

All-purpose flour

Seasoning salt

Shortening

1 (10¾-ounce) can
condensed onion soup

½ can beer

Cut the steak in serving-size pieces. Soak overnight in the salted water in the refrigerator. Roll the steak pieces in a mixture of the flour and seasoning salt. Brown steak lightly on both sides in the shortening over medium heat. Drain off the grease. Mix the soup and beer, and pour over the steak. Cover and simmer for 45 to 50 minutes.

SERVINGS WILL DEPEND ON THE SIZE OF THE STEAK.

Dad's Favorite Smothered Venison

Lisa Burns
Portland, Tennessee

This is my hunter's favorite.

—LISA BURNS

2 cups all-purpose flour

Salt

Garlic powder

1 cup milk

1 egg

Venison steak or tenderloin

1½ cups peanut oil

1 onion, sliced in rings

2 cups mushrooms

Mix the flour, salt, garlic powder, milk, and egg in a large bowl. Add the steak or tenderloin to this mixture, and coat it well. Let stand for 30 minutes to 1 hour in the refrigerator. Brown the meat on both sides in the oil. Then in a skillet, layer the onion rings on the bottom, put in the browned meat, and then the mushrooms on top. Add water to cover the meat. Let this come to a boil, and then put a lid on the skillet to finish cooking to your own taste.

SERVINGS WILL DEPEND ON THE SIZE OF THE STEAK.

Venison Kabobs

Cindy Hill
Smyrna, Tennessee

2 large venison round steaks, cubed

1 (8-ounce) bottle French dressing

1 pound mushrooms

2 large onions, cubed

2 bell peppers, cubed

1 (20-ounce) can pineapple chunks

1 (6-ounce) can water chestnuts

Marinate the cubed venison in the French dressing overnight in the refrigerator. Skewer the meat, alternating with the mushrooms, onions, bell peppers, pineapple, and water chestnuts. Grill on low coals, and baste frequently. Cook for 15 minutes on each side. Serve over rice.

MAKES 6 TO 8 SERVINGS.

Barbecued Venison Sandwiches

Mrs. Gary Pollitt
Cookeville, Tennessee

1 cup catsup

¼ cup vinegar

2 tablespoons chopped onions

1 tablespoon Worcestershire sauce

2 teaspoons brown sugar

¼ teaspoon dry mustard

1 garlic clove, crushed

3 cups 1-inch slices venison

6 hamburger buns

Heat the catsup, vinegar, onions, Worcestershire sauce, brown sugar, dry mustard, and garlic to boiling over medium heat, stirring constantly. Reduce the heat, and stir in the venison slices. Cover and simmer until the venison is hot, about 15 minutes. Fill the hamburger buns with the mixture. Serve with French fries and coleslaw.

MAKES 6 SERVINGS.

Make a deer-hauling harness from a 3 x 16-inch piece of heavy leather with a slightly larger strip of carpet glued to one side for padding. Punch holes near each end of the leather strip, and pass a 12-foot-long rope through them. Tie the end to your deer's antlers, place the leather strip across the back of your neck, and pass the ropes under your arms. Lean your weight into the harness, and the padded leather strip will settle across the top of your shoulders.

Venison Pepper Steak

Mary Sims

1   pound deer steak, cut ¼-inch thick

Salt water

2   tablespoons fat

¼   cup chopped onion

1   garlic clove, minced

1   bell pepper, cut in thin strips or rings

1   teaspoon salt

Dash of pepper

1   cube beef bouillon

1   cup hot water

2   tablespoons soy sauce

2   tablespoons cornstarch

¼   cup cold water

1   pound chopped tomatoes (optional)

Soak the deer in salt water for 8 to 12 hours in the refrigerator. Rinse, cut meat in finger-size pieces, and brown in fat. Add the onion, garlic, and bell pepper. Season with the salt and pepper. Dissolve the bouillon cube in the hot water, and add to meat. Cover, and simmer until the meat is tender, 20 to 25 minutes. Combine the soy sauce, cornstarch, and cold water, and stir into the meat mixture. Simmer until the gravy thickens. Remove the garlic. One pound of tomatoes can be added at the same time as the cornstarch mixture. Serve over hot noodles or mashed potatoes and homemade biscuits.

MAKES 4 SERVINGS.

Venison Pepper Steak with Mushrooms

Mrs. Gary Pollitt
Cookeville, Tennessee

1	pound venison steak
¼	cup all-purpose flour
1	teaspoon salt
¼	cup vegetable oil
2	medium green peppers
1	medium onion
2	(3-ounce) cans sliced mushrooms
1	tablespoon soy sauce
1	cup water

Cut the venison steak into 2-inch strips. Toss the strips in a mixture of the flour and salt. Heat the oil in a 10-inch skillet. Fry the steak until brown, and remove from the skillet. Cut the green peppers into 1-inch pieces; cut the onion into ¾-inch pieces. Put the peppers and onions in the skillet, and add the mushrooms, soy sauce, and water. Heat to a boil over medium heat, stirring constantly, and then reduce the heat. Add the venison to the vegetables, and let simmer about 1 hour. For a thicker gravy, add a mixture of cornstarch and water and stir. Serve over cooked rice.

MAKES 4 SERVINGS.

Venison Stroganoff

William & Andrea Bolden
Unionville, Tennessee

	Venison steaks (about 1 pound)
1	onion, chopped
	Oil
1	(10¾-ounce) can condensed golden mushroom soup
1	(4-ounce) can sliced mushrooms
1	(8-ounce) carton sour cream

Cut the steaks into bite-size pieces, and brown with the onion in a skillet with a little oil. When browned, stir in the soup and mushrooms. Simmer until the steaks are tender. Stir in the sour cream, and serve over cooked rice or noodles.

MAKES 2 TO 3 SERVINGS.

Venison Steak Casserole

Mrs. James R. Miller

2 pounds venison steak, cut ³/₄ inch thick

6 tablespoons all-purpose flour

Salt and pepper

1 garlic clove, crushed

¹/₈ teaspoon oregano

Shortening

4 medium potatoes, thinly sliced

2 medium onions, sliced

2 carrots, sliced

3 cups beef bouillon

1 green pepper, cut in rings

Tenderize the steak, and roll in part of the flour seasoned with salt, pepper, garlic, and oregano. Brown in the shortening. Preheat the oven to 350 degrees. Place the steak in the bottom of a baking dish. Layer half of the potatoes, onions, and carrots on top, and sprinkle with the remaining seasoned flour. Layer the remaining half of the potatoes, onions, and carrots over the flour. Pour the bouillon over the top of the vegetables, and add the pepper rings. Cover and bake in the oven for 1 hour, or until the vegetables are done.

MAKES 4 TO 6 SERVINGS.

Venison and Rice Casserole

William & Andrea Bolden
Unionville, Tennessee

1 onion, chopped

1 green pepper, chopped

1¹/₂ pounds venison, cut in bite-size pieces

2 tablespoons shortening

2 teaspoons salt

1 tablespoon brown sugar

3 cups canned tomatoes, undrained

1 cup rice, uncooked

Sauté the onion, green pepper, and venison in the shortening in a skillet until browned. Add the salt, brown sugar, tomatoes, and rice; mix well. Preheat the oven to 325 degrees. Pour the venison mixture into a casserole, and bake for 1 hour.

MAKES 6 TO 8 SERVINGS.

When seeing an alert deer, remember that deer have an attention span of about three minutes. If you come up to an alert deer, or you make a motion or noise that alerts a deer, wait motionless and silently for about three minutes—by then the deer should have forgotten your mistake.

Venison Stew

Maureen Irons
Charlotte, Tennessee

1   **pound venison, cubed**

1   **(15-ounce) can crushed tomatoes, or freshly grown, tomatoes, chopped**

1   **large onion, chopped**

2 or 3 **celery ribs, chopped**

2   **large potatoes, peeled and sliced**

3   **carrots, scraped and sliced**

2   **teaspoons instant bouillon**

$^{1}/_{2}$ **cup water**

$^{1}/_{4}$ **cup chopped parsley**

$^{1}/_{4}$ **cup wine (optional)**

Salt and pepper

Place the venison, tomatoes, onion, celery, potatoes, carrots, bouillon, water, parsley, and wine in a large Dutch oven or pot. Cook for 1 hour over medium heat. Simmer for 6 to 8 hours. Season with salt and pepper to taste.

MAKES 4 TO 6 SERVINGS.

Crock-Pot Venison Stew

William & Andrea Bolden
Unionville, Tennessee

Salt and pepper
2   **pounds venison stew meat**
2   **tablespoons butter**
½   **cup onion, chopped**
2   **teaspoons garlic powder**
½   **cup water**
½   **cup red wine**
1   **(8-ounce) can tomato sauce**
3   **potatoes, peeled and sliced**
3   **carrots, peeled and sliced**

Salt and pepper the venison cubes to taste. Brown them lightly in the butter in a skillet, and then transfer the venison to a Crock-Pot. Add the onion, garlic powder, water, red wine, tomato sauce, potatoes, and carrots to the Crock-Pot, and cook on low for 10 hours.

MAKES 6 TO 8 SERVINGS.

Easy Crock-Pot Venison Stew

Frank & Wanda Chum
Franklin, Tennessee

1½ **pounds venison steak,**
    cut into 1- or 2-inch cubes
1   **(12-ounce) can mixed**
    vegetables, drained
1   **(12-ounce) can whole kernel**
    corn, drained
1   **(16-ounce) can tomatoes**
1   **(6-ounce) can tomato paste**
1   **onion, chopped**
3   **(3-ounce) cans sliced**
    mushrooms
    Dash of salt

Put the venison steak, mixed vegetables, corn, tomatoes, tomato paste, onion, mushrooms, and salt in a Crock-Pot. Cook 8 to 10 hours on high.

MAKES 6 TO 8 SERVINGS.

Bugs and Deer Stew

1 **pound package black beans**

1 **(28- to 32-ounce) jar of salsa**

1 **pound ground venison**
Hot sauce

Cook the beans according to the package directions. In a large skillet, brown the meat. To the beans, add the salsa, venison, and hot sauce to taste. Cook over medium heat until hot. Serve with nachos or corn chips, or corn or flour tortillas.

MAKES 4 SERVINGS.

Hunter's Stew

Patsy Graves
Bethpage, Tennessee

2 **pounds lean venison**

1 **soup bone (shank)**

½ **pound suet**

4 **ribs celery**

3 **onions, chopped**

1½ **gallons cold water**

1½ **cups peas**

1½ **cups corn**

1½ **cups tomatoes**

1½ **cups lima beans**

5 **potatoes, diced**

1½ **carrots, diced**

¼ **cup rice**

¼ **cup chili sauce**

Combine the meat, soup bone, suet, celery, onion, and water. Simmer 2½ hours. Remove the celery and soup bone. Add the peas, corn, tomatoes, lima beans, potatoes, carrots, and rice, and simmer over low heat until vegetables are done. Before serving, season with the chili sauce, and more salt and pepper if needed. This is a thick stew.

MAKES 8 TO 10 SERVINGS.

In thick cover, you can get very close to animals that have not seen or smelled you, by sounding like a browsing deer. Since deer don't feed when they're nervous, the sounds a feeding deer makes are reassuring to other deer or game animals. Take a few steps, stop, and then pluck leaves sporadically from surrounding bushes. Tear the leaves from the branches with a yank, using your thumbnail to cut them off. Then take a few steps and repeat.

Venison, Elk, or Antelope Stew in a Pressure Cooker

Deborah Lynn Davis
Red Boiling Springs, Tennessee

Game meat of choice

2   **cups vinegar**

¼   **cup salt**

4   **medium onions, chopped**

   Black pepper

3   **cups catsup**

1   **pound carrots**

4   **medium potatoes, cubed**

1   **cup A.1. steak sauce**

Cut the game meat into 4 x 4-inch pieces. Place the meat in a large container, and pour water, vinegar, and salt over it. Soak for 24 hours in the refrigerator. Take the meat out and wash. Place in a pressure cooker with 2 of the onions, and season with pepper. Cook in the pressure cooker until done, but do not take the meat out of the cooker. Add 1 cup water, the catsup, the remaining 2 onions, and carrots. Add more black pepper. Cook on medium heat, and stir for 30 minutes. Add the potatoes, and let cook on high for 2 hours. When potatoes are tender, add A.1. sauce, and salt and pepper to taste. Turn the heat down, and let simmer for 20 minutes.

SERVINGS WILL DEPEND ON THE AMOUNT OF GAME USED.

Venison Ragout

Jerry B. Poyner
Brentwood, Tennessee

3   pounds venison

3   tablespoons olive oil

3   large onions, chopped

5   garlic cloves, crushed

½   pound bacon, chopped

1   teaspoon curry powder

1   (10¾-ounce) can condensed tomato soup

1½ quarts water

2   teaspoons bourbon

¼   cup beer

1   tablespoon salt

½   pound fresh mushrooms, sliced

3   tablespoons Worcestershire sauce

2   tablespoons butter or margarine

Cut the venison into 1-inch cubes. Heat the olive oil in a skillet, and add the venison, onions, garlic, and bacon. Cook until all are browned, stirring frequently. Add the curry powder, tomato soup, water, bourbon, beer, and salt. Cover and simmer for 50 minutes. In a separate pan, sauté the mushrooms with Worcestershire sauce and butter. Add the mushrooms to the meat mixture, and simmer for 10 minutes more. Serve over rice.

MAKES 8 SERVINGS.

The first step toward tree-stand safety is good tree selection. A safe tree is healthy and fully alive. Dead or partially dead trees are dangerous. Straight trees are safest.

Venison Chili

Becky and Mark Arnold
Bruceton, Tennessee

2 pounds ground venison

¼ cup vegetable oil

1 cup onions, chopped

2 garlic cloves, minced

1 large green pepper, cut in strips

3 tablespoons chili powder

2 teaspoons sugar

3½ cups canned whole tomatoes

1 cup tomato sauce

1 cup water

½ teaspoon salt

1 tablespoon all-purpose flour (optional)

2 tablespoons water (optional)

2 cups kidney beans

Mozzarella or cheddar cheese for topping (optional)

In a large iron skillet, brown the venison in the vegetable oil. Add the onions, garlic, and green pepper. Cook 5 minutes, stirring constantly. Add the chili powder, sugar, tomatoes, tomato sauce, water, and salt. If a thicker chili is desired, stir in the 1 tablespoon flour mixed with 2 tablespoons water. Just before serving, add the beans. Top with grated mozzarella or cheddar cheese if desired.

MAKES 6 TO 8 SERVINGS.

If you're a bow hunter, choose brightly colored vanes or feathers for your arrows. They're more visible when you try to find one on the ground and also easier to follow during flight.

Venison and Beef Chili

Andy and Betty Thomason
Columbia, Tennessee

2 pounds venison, cut into
  $\frac{1}{2}$ -inch cubes

1 pound ground beef

2 large red onions, chopped

2 (15$\frac{1}{2}$-ounce) cans
  kidney beans

3 (8-ounce cans) tomato sauce

1 (6-ounce) can tomato paste

1 cup water

3 to 4 tablespoons chili powder

1 pod red pepper

Combine the venison, ground beef, and onions in a large iron skillet. Cook until the meat is browned; drain off the fat. Stir in the beans, tomato sauce, tomato paste, water, chili powder, and red pepper. Cover and simmer for 1$\frac{1}{2}$ hours or until the venison is tender, adding water as needed.

MAKES ALMOST A GALLON OF CHILI.

Jimmy's Venison Patties

2 pounds ground venison
  tenderloin

3 tablespoons very fine bread
  crumbs

2 tablespoons grated onion
  (optional)

2 teaspoons salt

1 egg, lightly beaten

$\frac{1}{2}$ teaspoon turmeric

$\frac{1}{4}$ teaspoon chili powder

$\frac{1}{4}$ teaspoon garlic salt
  (optional)

$\frac{1}{8}$ teaspoon pepper

$\frac{1}{2}$ cup margarine or clear
  bacon fat

$\frac{1}{3}$ cup water

Blend the deer tenderloin, bread crumbs, onion, salt, egg, turmeric, chili powder, garlic salt, and pepper thoroughly, leaving out the garlic or onion if you prefer. Shape into patties. Brown the patties in the margarine or bacon fat. When browned, add the water and cover. Simmer 1 hour and 30 minutes.

MAKES 4 TO 8 SERVINGS.

Barbecued Venison Burgers

Andy & Betty Thomason
Columbia, Tennessee

1   **pound ground venison**

½   **cup oatmeal**

½   **teaspoon salt**

¼   **teaspoon pepper**

½   **cup evaporated milk**

     Barbecue sauce
     (recipe follows)

Mix the venison, oatmeal, salt, pepper, and evaporated milk. Let the meat mixture flavors blend while you prepare the barbecue sauce. Brown the meat patties in a large iron skillet, and add the sauce. Let simmer for 30 to 40 minutes.

MAKES 4 SERVINGS.

Note:

This recipe also works well over a camp fire, or even in a Crock-Pot.

Barbecue Sauce

1   **tablespoon Worcestershire**
     sauce

½   **tablespoon vinegar**

1   **tablespoon sugar**

½   **cup catsup**

¼   **cup water**

1   **medium onion, finely**
     chopped

In a small bowl, mix the Worcestershire sauce, vinegar, sugar, catsup, water, and onion.

Venison Burgers Parmigiana

Gerry Szalay
Nashville, Tennessee

1	**pound ground or chopped venison**
½	**teaspoon garlic salt**
¼	**cup chopped onion**
1	**(8-ounce) can tomato sauce**
1	**cup grated mozzarella cheese**
1	**tablespoon parsley flakes**
1	**tablespoon oregano flakes**
2	**tablespoons bread crumbs**

Preheat the oven to 400 degrees. Mix the meat, garlic salt, and onion. Shape into 8 patties, and place in a well-greased baking dish. Pour the tomato sauce over the patties. Sprinkle with the cheese, parsley, oregano, and bread crumbs. Bake in the oven for about 30 minutes.

MAKES 4 TO 6 SERVINGS.

Barbecued Venison Sloppy Joes

Patsy Graves
Bethpage, Tennessee

8	**pounds ground venison**
2	**teaspoons salt**
½	**cup oil**
1½	**cups chopped onion**
1½	**cups chopped celery**
½	**cup brown sugar**
2	**tablespoons prepared mustard**
½	**cup vinegar**
2	**quarts tomato juice**

Brown the venison in a large heavy skillet, stirring to keep crumbly. Add the salt. In another skillet, heat the oil and sauté the onion and celery until tender. Add to the venison. Add the sugar, mustard, vinegar, and tomato juice, and simmer for 15 minutes. Serve on warm buns.

MAKES 50 SERVINGS.

Venison Burger and Noodle Bake

Christyne Wolfe
Lascassas, Tennessee

1	**pound ground venison**
1	**green pepper, chopped**
1	**onion, chopped**
	Salt and pepper
1	**tablespoon chili powder**
1	**(10¾-ounce) can condensed tomato soup**
1	**(10¾-ounce) can condensed cream of mushroom soup**
1	**(16-ounce) can cream-style corn**
1	**(16-ounce) package noodles, cooked**
1	**cup grated cheese**

Brown the venison, green pepper, and onions. Add the salt, pepper, chili powder, soups, corn, noodles, and cheese. Mix well. Preheat the oven to 325 degrees. Put the mixture in a baking dish, and sprinkle with more grated cheese. Bake in the oven until bubbly, 30 to 40 minutes.

MAKES 12 SERVINGS.

When driving deer, make sure the people pushing the woods move slowly. Sometimes mature bucks will simply hunker down and let you walk right past them if you move too quickly. Walking slowly and even pausing occasionally is a good idea, to unnerve any deer hidden in brush or lying next to a blow-down.

Venison Burger and Eggplant Casserole

Mrs. James R. Miller

1 large eggplant, about a pound

Salt and pepper

3 tablespoons lemon juice

1 onion, chopped

1 pound ground venison

¼ pound (1 stick) butter or margarine

1 garlic clove, crushed

1 green pepper, chopped

1 cup beef stock

Dash of claret wine

Dash of celery salt

Dash of oregano

½ cup cooked rice

All-purpose flour

¼ cup olive or corn oil

2 tablespoons butter or margarine

2 eggs, beaten

1 tablespoon chopped parsley

¼ cup grated Parmesan cheese

Wash and cut the eggplant into ½-inch-thick slices, salt and pepper each slice, and sprinkle ½ of the lemon juice over them. Using a heavy pot, sauté the onion, venison, garlic, and green pepper in 3 tablespoons of the butter or margarine. Cook for 10 minutes. Season with salt and pepper while cooking, and add the rest of the lemon juice, the beef stock, and wine. Cook 10 more minutes. Add the celery salt, oregano, and rice. Mix well and remove from the heat. Roll the eggplant slices in the flour, and fry in oil and butter or margarine. When browned, place half of the eggplant slices in the bottom of a 9 x 14-inch pan. Mix the eggs with the meat mixture, spread over the eggplant in the pan, and sprinkle with the parsley. Place the rest of the eggplant slices over the top, and sprinkle with the cheese. Preheat the oven to 350 degrees. Place the eggplant pan inside a larger pan containing ½ inch of water. Bake 1 hour, adding more liquid if the eggplant becomes too dry. Keep the pan covered while baking.

MAKES 6 TO 8 SERVINGS.

Venison Meat Loaf

Mrs. Gary Pollitt
Cookeville, Tennessee

2   **pounds ground venison**

½   **cup finely cut onion**

½   **cup finely cut celery**

2   **eggs, beaten**

24 **crackers, finely crumbled**

¼   **cup milk**

¼   **cup catsup**

½   **teaspoon salt**
    Pepper

1   **(8-ounce) can mushrooms**

Preheat the oven to 350 degrees. Mix the venison, onion, celery, eggs, crackers, milk, catsup, salt, pepper to taste, and mushrooms together. Pack the mixture into a 9 x 4-inch loaf pan. Top with more catsup and mushrooms. Bake in the oven 1¼ hours.

MAKES 6 TO 8 SERVINGS.

Gary's Favorite Venison Spaghetti

Mrs. Gary Pollitt
Cookeville, Tennessee

1   **pound ground venison**

1   **large onion, chopped**

1   **garlic clove, crushed**

1   **cup water**

1   **teaspoon salt**

1   **teaspoon sugar**

1   **teaspoon oregano**

¾   **teaspoon basil**

½   **teaspoon marjoram**

1   **(8-ounce) can mushrooms**

1   **(8-ounce) can tomato sauce**

1   **(8-ounce) can tomato paste**

1   **(16-ounce) package spaghetti**
    Parmesan cheese (optional)

Cook and stir the venison, onions, and garlic until the meat is light brown; drain. Stir in the water, salt, sugar, oregano, basil, marjoram, mushrooms, tomato sauce, and tomato paste. Heat to boiling and reduce heat. Cover and let simmer 2 hours, stirring occasionally. Cook the spaghetti according to package directions. Serve the sauce over hot spaghetti, and sprinkle with Parmesan cheese if desired.

MAKES 4 TO 6 SERVINGS.

Venison Meatball Pot Pie

Kenny Brown
Burkesville, Kentucky

1	**(9-inch) piecrust, unbaked**
1	**(5$\frac{1}{2}$-ounce) package au gratin potatoes**
1	**(10-ounce) package frozen peas and carrots, thawed and drained**
1	**pound ground venison**
1	**cup soft bread crumbs**
$\frac{1}{4}$	**cup milk**
1	**egg**
2	**tablespoons chopped parsley**
2	**tablespoons chopped onion**
$\frac{1}{2}$	**teaspoon salt**
$\frac{1}{8}$	**teaspoon pepper**

Let the piecrust get to room temperature. Prepare the potatoes in a 2-quart casserole, according to package directions, but omitting the butter. Stir in the peas and carrots. Combine the venison, bread crumbs, milk, egg, parsley, onion, salt, and pepper in a mixing bowl. Shape into 1$\frac{1}{2}$-inch balls, and place on top of the potato mixture. Cover the top of the casserole with the piecrust, trim, and fold under. Seal the edge of the pastry, cutting slits to let steam escape. Preheat the oven to 375 degrees, and bake for 1$\frac{1}{4}$ hours or until potatoes are tender.

MAKES 4 TO 5 SERVINGS.

Venison Burrito Bake

Kenny Brown
Burkesville, Kentucky

1	**(16-ounce can) refried beans**
1	**cup biscuit baking mix**
$\frac{1}{4}$	**cup water**
1	**pound ground venison**
1	**cup thick salsa**
1$\frac{1}{2}$	**cups shredded cheddar cheese**
1	**avocado, sliced (optional)**
	Sour cream (optional)

Preheat the oven to 375 degrees. In a large iron skillet, brown the venison. In a large bowl, mix the beans, baking mix, and water very well. Spread the mixture in the bottom, and half way up the sides, of a greased, 10-inch pie plate. Add the venison, salsa, cheese, and avocado. Bake for 30 minutes. Place a dollop of sour cream on each serving, if desired.

MAKES 8 SERVINGS.

There is a saying that a deer thinks a hunter is a stump, and a turkey thinks a stump is a hunter.

Microwave Venison Pie

Kenny Brown
Burkesville, Kentucky

1 package spaghetti sauce mix

1 (6-ounce) can tomato paste

1¾ cups hot water

2 tablespoons butter or oil

½ cup finely crumbled dry bread crumbs

1 teaspoon garlic salt

1½ pounds ground venison

1 (4-ounce) package shredded cheddar or mozzarella cheese

½ teaspoon oregano

3 tablespoons grated Parmesan cheese

In a 1-quart bowl, combine the spaghetti sauce mix and tomato paste. Add the hot water and butter. Cover with waxed paper and microwave on high setting for 15 minutes, stirring every 4 minutes. In a 10-inch pie plate, combine the bread crumbs, garlic salt, meat, and ½ cup sauce. Press the mixture evenly across the bottom and sides of the pie plate. Microwave on high for 8 to 9 minutes, turning the dish one-half turn after 4 minutes. Drain off any fat. Spread the remaining sauce on top of the meat. Top with the cheddar cheese, oregano, and Parmesan cheese. Microwave on high for 3 to 4 minutes.

MAKES 6 SERVINGS.

Note:

For the conventional oven, assemble pie as directed, and bake in a 375-degree oven for 25 minutes.

Stuffed Grape Leaves

Patsy Graves
Bethpage, Tennessee

12 large grape leaves
    Water
½ pound ground venison
1 minced medium onion
2 tablespoons vegetable oil
1 teaspoon grated lemon rind
1 teaspoon salt
⅛ teaspoon pepper
½ cup white raisins
2 cups cooked rice
1 cup water

Grease a 1½-quart casserole. Wash grape leaves. Blanch the grape leaves in boiling water for 30 seconds. Drain leaves, plunge in cold water, drain again, and set aside. In a large skillet, brown the ground venison and onion in oil. Stir in the lemon rind, salt, pepper, raisins, and rice. Preheat the oven to 350 degrees. Place ⅓ cup of filling on each leaf. Fold the leaves around the filling. Place in the casserole with folded sides down. Add 1 cup water. Cover and bake for 20 to 30 minutes, until the liquid is almost gone.

MAKES 4 SERVINGS.

Hickory Stick Venison

David Grech
Hermitage, Tennessee

David stopped me in Rivergate Mall to tell me about this Hickory Stick recipe. He says it's tasty. Deer hunters will probably love it. —JIMMY

5 pounds ground venison or hamburger
5 rounded teaspoons curing salt (Morton Tender Quick)
2½ teaspoons mustard seed
2½ teaspoons black pepper
2½ teaspoons garlic salt
1 teaspoon hickory smoked salt

Thoroughly mix the venison, curing salt, mustard seed, black pepper, garlic salt, and hickory smoked salt; cover and refrigerate. For 3 days, remove from the refrigerator once a day and mix. On the fourth day, form the meat into rolls, and lay them on a rack or broiler pan. Bake at 175 degrees for 8 hours. The hickory sticks form their own coating.

MAKES 10 TO 12 SERVINGS.

When scouting in the early season for big deer, don't spend too much time watching over fields. Walk around the food sources, and look for large tracks after a rain. You'll spend less time in the woods. Scout for a spot for about a month before the season to learn where deer like to eat and rest. Put a tree stand by a place they feed, like an apple orchard.

Venison Jerky

Maureen Irons
Charlotte, Tennessee

1½ pounds venison flank steak or backstrap

½ teaspoon seasoned salt

⅓ teaspoon pepper

¼ cup soy sauce

1 teaspoon monosodium glutamate

⅓ teaspoon onion powder

¼ cup Worcestershire sauce

Trim all the fat from the venison, and partially freeze the meat. Slice the meat with the grain, cutting strips 2 inches long and ½ inch thick. Place the meat in a shallow pan. Combine the seasoned salt, pepper, soy sauce, monosodium glutamate, onion powder, and Worcestershire sauce; pour over the meat. Be sure to cover the venison well, and let it sit overnight in the refrigerator. The next morning, start up the fire and make some smoldering coals. Place an airtight smoker over your fire. Place the strips on the rack in your smoker, or lay the strips of marinated meat in a single layer on the oven rack with foil underneath to catch the drippings. Leave the oven door open a crack. Bake the meat at 200 degrees for 8 to 12 hours or until chewy. Test by tasting. Store in an airtight container or keep covered.

MAKES 6 SERVINGS.

Orange-Onion Deer Liver

Mildred Curle
Nashville, Tennessee

¹/₄ **cup all-purpose flour**

¹/₈ **teaspoon salt**

¹/₈ **teaspoon pepper**

1 **pound deer, antelope, elk, or moose liver, trimmed and sliced ¹/₂ inch thick**

¹/₂ **cup butter or margarine**

1 **medium yellow onion, thinly sliced**

1 **medium red onion, thinly sliced**

1 **tablespoon sugar**

1 **medium orange, sliced**

¹/₃ **cup venison stock or beef broth**

¹/₄ **cup brandy**

¹/₄ **teaspoon dried thyme leaves**

Preheat the oven to 175 degrees. On a sheet of waxed paper, mix the flour, salt, and pepper. Dip the liver slices in the flour mixture, turning to coat. In a large skillet, melt ¹/₄ cup of the butter over medium heat. Add the liver slices, and brown on both sides. With a slotted spoon, transfer to a heated serving platter. Keep warm in the oven. Add the onions to the butter in the skillet. Cook and stir over medium heat until tender. Set aside and keep warm. Put the sugar on a sheet of waxed paper, and coat orange slices on both sides. In a medium skillet, melt the remaining ¹/₄ cup butter over medium heat. Add the orange slices. Fry until golden brown, turning once. Remove the orange slices. Add the stock, brandy, and thyme to the butter in the skillet. Cook over low heat for 5 minutes, stirring constantly. Remove from the heat. To serve, arrange the onions over the liver slices. Pour the broth mixture over the onions and liver. Top with the orange slices.

MAKES 3 OR 4 SERVINGS.

Venison is very low in cholesterol. A 3.6-ounce cut of chicken with skin has 83 milligrams of cholesterol, ground beef has 85, pork has 101, and venison has 66.

— ANTELOPE —

Antelope Steak

I got this recipe from a wild game dinner in Sumner County. Not many antelope here in the great state of Tennessee, but some folks get to go to exotic places to hunt. I suppose you could substitute venison.

—JIMMY

2   tablespoons shortening

4   tablespoons flour

2   pounds 1-inch-thick antelope steak, cut in serving pieces

2   soup cans water

   Salt and pepper

1   (10¾-ounce) can condensed cream of mushroom soup

1   cup diced celery

¼   cup diced onions

1   (4-ounce) can mushroom slices, drained

Heat the shortening in a skillet, pound the flour into the meat, and brown well. Pour in 1 soup can water, and simmer for half an hour. Add the salt and pepper. Mix together the soup and the remaining water, and pour on the meat. Add the celery, onions, and mushrooms, and cook on low heat for 1 hour. Fluffy, riced potatoes with snipped parsley for color, and shoe peg corn with pimiento will round out this meal.

MAKES 6 TO 8 SERVINGS.

— BEAR —

I've had the pleasure of being invited to many wild game dinners, and every once in a while I pick up some good recipes. I may have more recipes for bear than you'll need, but bear populations, and hunters, have increased a lot over the last decade.

If you see a bear is moving hurriedly, don't waste your time following it, but note where you last saw it. The bear may reappear in the same vicinity within a few hours or the next day.

Bear Roast

John Scarbrough
Tullahoma, Tennessee

1   (4-pound) bear roast, fat removed
    Apple cider vinegar
2   garlic cloves, sliced
    Salt and pepper
    Bacon slices
1   large onion, chopped
1   rib celery, chopped
3   teaspoons all-purpose flour
2 to 3 cups water
2   teaspoons sage leaves, crushed
1   dash Worcestershire sauce
    Various herbs (optional)

Place the roast in a pan, and cover with apple cider vinegar; let sit in the refrigerator overnight. Preheat the oven to 450 degrees. Cut slits in the roast, and insert garlic, salt, and pepper to taste. Place a few bacon slices in a roasting pan and place the meat on top of them. Cook in the oven for 15 minutes, then at 300 degrees for 2 hours. Remove 2 or 3 tablespoons of fat from the pan. In a large skillet, cook the onion and celery in the fat until the onions are translucent. Add the flour and mix with the fat. Add the water, and stir to make a gravy. Cook for a few minutes; then add the sage and Worcestershire sauce, and simmer until thick. Stir to keep from sticking. Other herbs can be added according to taste.

MAKES 8 TO 10 SERVINGS.

Barbecued Bear

1 ½ pounds boneless bear meat

Bacon strips

Barbecue sauce (recipe follows)

Parboil the bear meat in water to cover, allowing about 10 minutes per pound. Prepare the barbecue sauce while the meat is cooking. Place several strips of bacon in a Dutch oven, deep-fat fryer, or large pot, and sauté. Then brown the meat on all sides. Add the barbecue sauce, and simmer with the meat over medium heat for at least 30 minutes, or until tender.

MAKES 4 TO 6 SERVINGS.

Barbecue Sauce

½ cup water

½ cup tomato sauce

2 medium onions, sliced

⅛ teaspoon garlic powder

2 teaspoons brown sugar

¼ teaspoon dried mustard

2 tablespoons lemon juice

2 tablespoons vinegar

2 tablespoons catsup

1 tablespoon Worcestershire sauce

In a medium bowl, mix the water, tomato sauce, onions, garlic powder, brown sugar, dried mustard, lemon juice, vinegar, catsup, and Worcestershire sauce. Simmer for 10 minutes.

Wined Bear Pot Roast

Arnold Williams's wild game dinner in Rutherford County

2   **cups dry red wine**

1   **cup canned broth**

2   **medium onions, sliced**

2   **cloves garlic, chopped**

2   **bay leaves**

2   **cloves**

¼   **teaspoon oregano**

¼   **teaspoon celery seeds**

¼   **teaspoon freshly cracked white peppercorns**

1   **teaspoon salt**

4   **pounds choice bear roast**

    Bacon drippings

Mix the wine, broth, onions, garlic, bay leaves, cloves, oregano, celery seeds, peppercorns, and salt. Pour the marinade over the meat, and let stand 3 to 4 days in the refrigerator. Turn the meat every day. Take the meat out of the marinade and drain well. Sear in the hot bacon drippings until browned on all sides. Put in a pan that has a tight cover, pour the marinade over the meat, and bring to a boil. Then simmer 2 hours, cooking until thick. Strain the liquid into a bowl. Skim off the fat. Mix 3 tablespoons of fat with 3 tablespoons of flour, add to the hot liquid, and cook 2 to 3 minutes. Add salt, if needed. Pour the gravy over the meat and keep in the covered pan until ready to serve.

MAKES 8 TO 10 SERVINGS.

Braised Bear Steak

    All-purpose flour

    Salt and pepper

    Thyme

2   **3-inch-thick bear steaks**

1   **cup sliced onions**

4   **tablespoons bacon fat**

1   **cup red wine**

2   **tablespoons tomato paste**

    Boiled potatoes

    Parsley for garnish

    Sautéed mushrooms

Pound the flour, salt, pepper, and thyme into the steak with a meat hammer. Brown the onions in the bacon fat, and add the meat. Brown the meat well on all sides. Add the wine and bring to a boil. Cook briskly for 5 minutes. Turn the steak, reduce heat, and cover the pan. Simmer for 1 to 1½ hours, adding more broth if necessary. When the steak is tender, remove it to a hot platter. Add the tomato paste and additional liquid, if needed, to the pan juices to make a smooth sauce. Taste for seasoning, and pour the sauce over the steak. Surround with the boiled potatoes, garnish with the parsley, and serve with the sautéed mushrooms.

MAKES 4 SERVINGS.

Country-Style Bear

Bear meat

Seasoned all-purpose flour

Oil

Seasonings

Dehydrated onion soup mix
or fresh onions (optional)

Slice the bear meat into serving-size portions, about ¼-inch thick. Tenderize with a meat hammer. Dredge in the seasoned flour. Brown quickly in a small amount of oil. Add enough water to cover the meat. Cover the pot tightly, and simmer until tender over low heat. Thicken the gravy to desired consistency with flour. Season to taste. Dehydrated onion soup or fresh onions may be used to add flavor.

SERVINGS WILL DEPEND ON THE SIZE OF THE BEAR MEAT.

— BOAR —

Pot Roast of Boar

Here's a wild boar recipe from East Tennessee, where I once taped a show on a hunting preserve. —JIMMY

Boar shoulder roast

Salted water

3   cups apple cider

2   onions, sliced

2   carrots, sliced

½   cup sliced celery

½   teaspoon dry sage

Simmer the meat in the salted water to cover for 1½ hours. Drain and return to the kettle with the apple cider, onions, carrots, celery, and dry sage. Cover and simmer until tender. Slice the meat, and arrange on a hot platter to keep warm. Make a gravy from the cooking liquid by adding a flour and water paste. Serve with buttered noodles.

SERVINGS WILL DEPEND ON THE SIZE OF THE ROAST.

Chapter 8

Marinades, Sauces, and Gravies

— MARINADES —

Almost everyone who enjoys wild game and fish has his or her own special marinades. Some very good cooks have told me that you can never underestimate the power of a marinade. Every marinade contains varying amounts of seasonings, sometimes oil, and always an acid. There are secrets, however, as to how these aromatic tenderizing liquids are kept and secrets as to how they can be abused.

Years ago I learned that marinades need to be kept in containers made of glass or impervious metal, like stainless steel; this is because the acid in the marinade can leach unwanted substances and flavors from porous containers. I also discovered that less marinade is needed to cover your game if the meat is placed in a container just large enough to hold it. Use a wooden spoon to stir or turn the meat occasionally.

When I learned how marinades spread flavor to meats, especially venison, I found a whole new world of taste. The amount of time you soak the meat in a marinade may vary from only a few minutes to many hours—I personally believe you learn the best timing for this process through experience.

Stronger, spicier marinades may be devised to make bland meats and other food more interesting, and I've had fun trying all kinds of different marinades on meats and other foods.

To me the most important function of a marinade is to tenderize tough foods. Sometimes marinades contain extract of papaya, a tenderizing agent.

Marinades can be cooked or uncooked. Cooked marinades more effectively impart their flavors to foods, and they are preferable if the soaking is to exceed 12 hours. Liquid marinades should be cooked in advance and thoroughly chilled before the food

135

is immersed. I've been told that the amount of vinegar should be reduced slightly if the meat is to be marinated longer than 24 hours.

The effects of marinating are hastened by higher temperatures, but so is the danger of bacterial activity. Refrigerate any foods in their marinade if the immersion period indicated is an hour or more. You can use both cooked and uncooked marinades as finishing sauces. So do not discard a marinade if you want to incorporate it in your sauce.

According to what I've learned over the years about cooking wild game and fish, you need to allow about ½ cup marinade for every pound of food to be processed. Cubed meat is soaked just 2 to 3 hours; a whole 5- to 10-pound piece of meat needs to be soaked overnight. Marinating 12 hours or more cuts the cooking time by one-third. Longer soaking times may make the marinade too pungent, killing the flavor of the meat.

In an emergency, try mixing oil and vinegar with packaged salad seasonings to achieve a quickly prepared marinade for meats or vegetables. You can't beat Italian dressing when it comes to marinating meats of all kinds.

Jimmy's Venison or Rabbit Marinade

1 cup chopped celery

1 cup chopped carrots

1 cup chopped onions

1½ cups vegetable oil

3 cups vinegar

2 cups water

½ cup coarsely chopped parsley

3 bay leaves

1 tablespoon thyme

1 tablespoon basil

1 tablespoon cloves

1 tablespoon allspice berries

Pinch of mace

1 tablespoon crushed peppercorns

6 crushed garlic cloves

Sauté the celery, carrots, and onions in the vegetable oil until the onions are golden. Then add the vinegar, water, parsley, bay leaves, thyme, basil, cloves, allspice berries, mace, peppercorns, and garlic. Simmer for 1 hour. Strain and cool. This marinade can be cooked and stored in the refrigerator and used as needed for venison and rabbit.

MAKES 8 TO 10 CUPS.

Soy-Sesame Seed Marinade

This fast, simple recipe is delicious on game or broiled or cooked fish.   —JIMMY

$^1\!/_2$ **cup soy sauce**

$^1\!/_2$ **cup minced onions**

2 **tablespoons sesame seeds**

2 **tablespoons salad oil**

2 **teaspoons salt**

2 **tablespoons light brown sugar**

2 **teaspoons lemon juice**

$^1\!/_2$ **teaspoon pepper**

$^1\!/_2$ **teaspoon ginger**

Combine the soy sauce, onions, sesame seeds, salad oil, salt, sugar, lemon juice, pepper, and ginger in a medium bowl.

MAKES ABOUT 1$^1\!/_2$ CUPS.

Strawberry Wine Marinade

Harry Boals
Hendersonville, Tennessee

This recipe can be used on wild game, fish, or store-bought vittles.
—HARRY BOALS

$^1\!/_2$ **cup strawberry wine**

$^3\!/_4$ **cup picante sauce**

2 to 3 teaspoons white vinegar

1 **tablespoon sorghum molasses**

Blend the strawberry wine, picante sauce, vinegar, and molasses. Cover the food to be cooked with the marinade. Use a brush to cover all the surfaces. Let stand 1 hour before placing on the grill. Cook the meat in the usual manner.

MAKES ABOUT 1$^1\!/_2$ CUPS.

Marinade to Tenderize Game Steaks

Hendersonville, Tennessee

The Italian dressing marinates the meat, making the most tender meat we have ever eaten. —HARRY BOALS

Seasoning salt

Lemon pepper

Garlic powder

½ bottle Italian dressing

Put the seasoning salt, lemon pepper, garlic powder, and Italian dressing in a gallon Ziploc bag; seal, covering the steaks, and refrigerate for 4 hours or overnight.

MAKES ½ CUP.

Wild Game Marinade

This is especially good for large animals with a strong, gamey taste. It's also good for mundane foods such as chops, steaks, or kabobs. —JIMMY

6 tablespoons lemon juice

2 teaspoons salt

½ cup water

½ teaspoon pepper

½ cup catsup

2 onions, sliced (optional)

1 teaspoon chili powder

1 garlic clove, minced

Mix the lemon juice, salt, water, pepper, catsup, onions, chili powder, and garlic. Marinate the wild game in the refrigerator for 48 hours, turning often. Cook on the grill.

MAKES ABOUT 2 CUPS.

Tennessee's Serious Marinade

This marinade will make most wild game tender. —JIMMY

¹⁄₃ **cup red wine or red wine vinegar**

¹⁄₄ **cup soy sauce**

¹⁄₄ **cup lemon juice**

¹⁄₄ **teaspoon dry mustard**

¹⁄₄ **teaspoon ginger**

1 **tablespoon sugar**

Mix the wine, soy sauce, lemon juice, mustard, ginger, and sugar. Marinate wild game in the refrigerator for 48 hours, turning often. Cook on the grill.

MAKES ABOUT 2 CUPS.

Sherry Marinade for Game

Debbie White

1 **package dry Italian dressing**

1 **cup cooking sherry**

¹⁄₂ **cup oil**

¹⁄₄ **cup soy sauce**

¹⁄₄ **cup Worcestershire sauce**

1 **large onion, diced**

Mix the Italian dressing, sherry, oil, soy sauce, Worcestershire sauce, and onion. Pour over the meat. Let stand in the refrigerator for 24 hours. Grill until done.

MAKES ABOUT 3 CUPS.

If a grouse flushes and you're caught off guard, don't waste an off-balance shot. Instead, plant your feet firmly, raise your gun, and get ready. Often a second, or even a third, bird will rocket out of the cover. If you don't waste a hasty shot on the initial bird, you'll have plenty of shells in your gun and be ready for the second or third grouse to flush.

Jimmy's Three Marinades for Fish

#1

2   tablespoons lemon juice

¼   cup olive oil

1   teaspoon salt

⅛   teaspoon pepper

Combine the lemon juice, olive oil, salt, and pepper. Marinate the fish, refrigerated and covered, for 2 to 3 hours. Turn frequently.

MAKES ⅓ CUP.

#2

½   teaspoon turmeric

½   teaspoon powdered ginger

1   small clove garlic, pressed

2 to 3 tablespoons lemon juice

½   teaspoon grated lemon rind

Combine the turmeric, ginger, garlic, lemon juice, and lemon rind. Toss the fish in this mixture, coating it thoroughly. Cover and refrigerate for 2 hours.

MAKES ¼ CUP.

#3

½   cup pineapple juice

2   teaspoons soy sauce

2   teaspoons lemon juice

1   clove garlic, minced

Combine the pineapple juice, soy sauce, lemon juice, and garlic. Marinate the fish, covered and refrigerated, for 2 hours. Turn frequently.

MAKES ABOUT ½ CUP.

You can make a simple marker buoy with a screw-top, quart-sized plastic bottle. Get 25 to 50 feet of thin nylon line, enough line to reach the depths you may fish. Tie one end to the neck of the bottle, and tie a heavy weight to the other end. Wrap the line around the bottle, and secure it with a heavy-duty rubber band.

Lemon-Butter Marinade

Here's a quick and easy marinade that I'm sure you'll enjoy on fish. —JIMMY

1 cup butter

⅓ cup lemon juice

¼ cup chopped parsley

1 tablespoon salt

1 tablespoon grated lemon peel

1 teaspoon sugar

¼ teaspoon pepper

Heat the butter in a saucepan over medium heat. Add the lemon juice, parsley, salt, lemon peel, sugar, and pepper, and stir until smooth.

MAKES ABOUT 1½ CUPS.

Red Wine Marinade for Game Birds

Harry Boals
Hendersonville, Tennessee

2 cups dry red wine

1 bunch scallions, sliced

1 clove garlic, minced

½ cup olive oil

¼ cup soy or teriyaki sauce

2 tablespoons dark brown sugar

1 teaspoon grated fresh ginger

1 tablespoon Worcestershire sauce

Mix the wine, scallions, garlic, olive oil, soy sauce, brown sugar, ginger, and Worcestershire sauce. Use the mixture for a marinade, or boil it for 10 minutes to use as a basting sauce.

MAKES ABOUT 3 CUPS.

Spicy-Hot Marinade for Game Birds

4 green onions

2 jalapeños or serranos, seeded

⅓ cup lemon juice

¼ cup honey

2 tablespoons vegetable oil

2 tablespoons fresh thyme leaves, or 2 teaspoons dried thyme

½ teaspoon salt

¼ teaspoon ground allspice

¼ teaspoon nutmeg

Place the onions, jalapeños, lemon juice, honey, vegetable oil, thyme, salt, allspice, and nutmeg in a food processor or blender, and blend until smooth. Pour over game bird breasts and marinate in the refrigerator for 2 to 6 hours, but no longer than 6 hours. Grill the breasts and brush with the marinade.

MAKES ABOUT 1 CUP.

Brandied Marinade for Game Birds

½ cup brandy

¼ cup soy sauce

2 tablespoons unsulfured molasses

½ teaspoon Dijon mustard

1 tablespoon grated fresh ginger

½ cup dry white wine

Mix the brandy, soy sauce, molasses, mustard, ginger, and wine. Pour over the birds, and marinate for 2 to 6 hours. Broil or grill the birds, basting occasionally with the marinade.

MAKES ABOUT 2 CUPS.

— SAUCES —

Simple Sauce

Simple and good. —JIMMY

1 cup chili sauce

1 tablespoon fresh lime or lemon juice

½ teaspoon prepared horseradish

In a small serving bowl, blend the chili sauce, lime juice, and horseradish. Chill for at least 30 minutes to blend flavors.

MAKES 1 CUP.

White Sauce

This is a very basic white sauce. If I have no cream soups in the house, I make it to pour over noodles and that sort of thing. It also makes a great base for any cream soup you might wish to make. —JIMMY

2 tablespoons butter

2 tablespoons all-purpose flour

1 cup milk

¼ teaspoon salt

Dash of pepper (optional)

Melt the butter in a sauce pan, and blend in the flour. Add the milk slowly, stirring constantly. Cook for 5 minutes. Add the salt and pepper.

MAKES 1¼ CUPS.

Variation:

Depending on what I'm serving with the white sauce, I sometimes add other seasonings, such as paprika, herbal seasoning, garlic, and onion. To make cream of mushroom soup, I add mushrooms, garlic, extra pepper, and a touch more milk. You can make other cream soups by adding chicken, turkey, roast beef, celery, peas, you name it.

Basic Tartar Sauce

1/2 cup mayonnaise or salad dressing

1/8 teaspoon salt

2 tablespoons chopped sweet pickle relish

2 tablespoons sour cream

2 tablespoons fresh lime or lemon juice

2 tablespoons finely chopped onion

Dash curry powder (optional)

Mix the mayonnaise, salt, pickle relish, sour cream, lime juice, onion, and curry powder in a small bowl. Chill for at least 30 minutes to blend flavors.

MAKES 1½ CUPS.

Saucy Tartar Sauce

1 cup mayonnaise

2 tablespoons finely chopped, drained, stuffed olives

1/4 cup sour cream

2 tablespoons finely chopped, drained dill pickle

1 teaspoon lemon juice

Dash of red pepper

2 tablespoons finely chopped onion

Combine the mayonnaise, olives, sour cream, dill pickle, lemon juice, red pepper, and onion; chill.

MAKES ABOUT 1½ CUPS.

Hotsy Totsy Tartar Sauce

1   cup mayonnaise

1   teaspoon Dijon mustard

1   teaspoon finely grated
    lemon zest

1   tablespoon fresh lemon juice
    Dash of Tabasco

2   tablespoons drained sweet
    pickle relish

2   tablespoons chopped flat-
    leaf parsley

2   tablespoons finely minced
    shallots

1   tablespoon drained tiny
    capers
    Salt and freshly ground
    black pepper

Combine the mayonnaise, mustard, lemon zest
and juice, Tabasco, and relish in a bowl. Stir in
the remaining ingredients. Refrigerate, covered,
at least 1 hour before serving, for flavors to
blend. Store refrigerated; it will last up to 3 days.

MAKES 2 CUPS.

Tangy Herb Sauce

³/₄ cup sour cream

3   tablespoons Dijon mustard

1   teaspoon basil

¹/₂ teaspoon onion powder

2   tablespoons finely chopped
    parsley

Mix the sour cream, mustard, basil, onion
powder, and parsley well, and serve over fish.

MAKES 1 CUP.

Lemon Parsley Sauce

Serve this tasty sauce over fish. —JIMMY

½ **stick butter, melted**

3 **tablespoons lemon juice**

1 **teaspoon grated lemon rind**

1 **tablespoon chopped parsley**

Melt the butter, and add the lemon juice, lemon rind, and parsley.

MAKES 1 CUP.

Apple Horseradish Sauce

This horseradish sauce goes well with trout. —JIMMY

4 **tablespoons drained and squeezed-dry prepared horseradish**

3 **tablespoons mayonnaise**

1 **tablespoon cider vinegar**

2 **teaspoons grainy mustard**

1 **teaspoon Dijon mustard**

1¼ **teaspoons sugar**

½ **teaspoon salt**

Dash of cayenne

2 **tablespoons finely chopped red onion**

¼ **Granny Smith apple with peel, cored and thinly sliced**

Whisk the horseradish, mayonnaise, cider vinegar, mustard, sugar, salt, and cayenne in a large bowl until well blended. Add the onion and apple, folding in gently. Refrigerate for several hours to allow the flavors to blend.

MAKES 2 CUPS.

When jump-shooting ducks along rivers and streams, try using a call every now and then. You might get birds that you hadn't seen to respond and reveal their location. At times they might even fly or swim down toward you into shooting range where you can flush them.

Delicious Duck Baste

Here's a recipe I found in my collection from Reelfoot Lake in Samburg, Tennessee. This one's good for ducks. —JIMMY

¼ **cup honey**

½ **cup soy sauce**

½ **cup sherry**

1 **garlic clove, finely minced**

1 **teaspoon freshly grated gingerroot, or ½ teaspoon ground ginger**

Combine the honey, soy sauce, sherry, garlic, and ginger in a saucepan; bring to a boil, and remove from the heat. Use the sauce to baste a duck every 15 minutes as it roasts or turns on the spit.

MAKES 1¼ CUPS.

Spicy Honey Mustard Sauce

Use this sauce for dipping or on sandwiches. It's great with chicken. —JIMMY

Honey

Mustard

Horseradish

Mix equal amounts of honey and mustard, and add horseradish to taste. Mix well.

— GRAVIES —

Brown Gravy

This is a quick recipe that goes well with most game. —JIMMY

2½ tablespoons solid vegetable
    oil
4   tablespoons flour
1   tablespoon chopped onion
1   small tomato
2   cups vegetable broth or
    water
    Salt

Put the oil in a frying pan, and, when hot, add the flour and stir constantly until brown. Add the chopped onion, and continue to stir for a few minutes. Add the tomato, and stir for 5 minutes, or until the liquid is almost evaporated (this will give the gravy a good flavor). Add a third of the broth or water, and stir until smooth and free from lumps. Add the rest of the liquid, and let boil slowly for 10 minutes. Strain and serve.

MAKES ABOUT 2 CUPS.

Cream Gravy for Game

Debbie White

    Pan drippings from wild
    game
2   teaspoons minced onion
2   tablespoons butter
2   teaspoons all-purpose flour
1½ cups heavy cream
2   teaspoons lemon juice
2   teaspoons tart jelly
    Salt

Pour the drippings from the pan in which the game has been roasted into a saucepan. Stir in the onion, butter, and flour, and cook 2 minutes. Slowly add the cream, cook, and stir until blended and thickened. Add the lemon juice and jelly, and cook until melted. Taste and season if necessary.

Egg Gravy

3 tablespoons solid vegetable shortening

1 egg, beaten

4½ tablespoons flour

2 cups milk or water

Salt

Heat the shortening in a skillet, and, when hot, add the egg and stir over the fire until it is a light brown color. Add the flour, and continue to stir until the flour is brown. Add a third of the milk or water, and stir until smooth and free from lumps. Add the remaining milk and bring to a boil. Salt to taste and serve.

MAKES 2½ CUPS.

Basic Pan Gravy

Pan drippings from a wild turkey

Melted unsalted butter, if needed

About 4 cups turkey stock or broth

¾ cup all-purpose flour

⅓ cup bourbon, port, or dry sherry (optional)

Pour the drippings from the roasting pan into a heat-proof glass bowl or large measuring cup. Let stand for 5 minutes, and then skim off and reserve the fat that rises to the top. Measure out ¾ cup of the fat, adding the melted butter, if needed. Add enough turkey stock to the skimmed pan drippings to make 6 cups total. Place the roasting pan over low heat on two burners of the stove and add the skimmed fat. Whisk in the flour, scraping up the browned bits on the bottom of the pan. Cook until lightly browned, about 2 minutes. Whisk in the pan drippings mixture, and bourbon, if desired. Cook, whisking often, until the gravy has thickened and is lump-free, about 5 minutes. Transfer to a warmed gravy boat and serve.

MAKES ABOUT 6 CUPS.

Decoys for snow geese can be made of white plastic garbage bags cut in a teardrop shape and stapled to wooden stakes that are in the shape of a "T." Wind gives the plastic shapes enticing movement.

Giblet Gravy

Giblets and neck of wild fowl

2 tablespoons chicken fat

2 tablespoons all-purpose flour

Salt and pepper

Place the giblets (liver, heart, and gizzard) and the neck in a saucepan, and cover them with cold water. Simmer slowly, and when the giblets are tender, remove the meat from the neck, and finely chop with the giblets, saving the water in which they were cooked. Heat the fat on top of the stove, and stir in the flour. Cook 2 minutes; then add 1 cup of the stock left from cooking the giblets, pouring it in gradually so as not to thin the gravy too much. If the gravy seems too thick, add a little hot water. Put in the chopped giblets and season to taste with salt and pepper.

MAKES ABOUT 1½ CUPS.

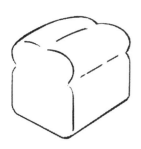

Chapter 9

Hush Puppies, Breads, and Stuffings

Becoming a successful cook is like any other undertaking—you have to have the right tools. Reading a recipe is easy enough, but getting those ingredients mixed thoroughly and in the right order is another thing. I have observed many professional cooks, and I have picked up many tips:

- When practical, prepare and measure out ingredients in advance of mixing or cooking.
- Preheat the oven to the specified temperature.
- Set the burners on the stoves to the proper temperature.
- Keep your kitchen organized.

— HUSH PUPPIES —

Dave's Hush Puppies

I got this terrific recipe from Dave Hughes, a fishing buddy of mine, many years ago. Dave got the recipe from someone around the Pickwick Dam area who ran a restaurant. These are the tastiest hush puppies you'll ever sink your teeth into. I promise you'll love them.

—JIMMY

1   cup self-rising flour
1   cup self-rising cornmeal
½   teaspoon baking powder
⅓   teaspoon baking soda
2   tablespoons sugar
1   egg
2   large onions, finely chopped
⅓   cup buttermilk
    Oil for frying

Mix the flour, cornmeal, baking powder, baking soda, sugar, egg, onions, and buttermilk well. Set the bowl aside, cover, and let the mixture rise (it won't be any huge rise, but it does lift a tad). Spoon a ball of the mixture, and gently place it into the hot oil. The hush puppies will brown beautifully; and when they are golden brown, take them out of the oil, and place them on a paper towel to soak up any extra oil.

MAKES ABOUT 4 TO 6 SERVINGS.

For you crappie fishermen, a great way to take crappies in summer is to fish at night under lights. Hang several lanterns over the side or use a foam-mounted light that floats on the water. Fish near weed beds, bends in the river channel, bridges, drop-offs, stumpy areas, or submerged islands. The light attracts insects and small bait fish. These in turn draw in predatory crappies. Use marabou jigs, soft plastic grubs, or small minnows fished 5 to 18 feet beneath a bobber.

Jimmy's Hush Puppies

I sometimes leave the corn out of this recipe and add more onions. —JIMMY

Vegetable oil for frying

1   cup yellow cornmeal

1/3   cup all-purpose flour

1   teaspoon sugar

1   teaspoon baking powder

1/8   teaspoon salt

1/8   teaspoon cayenne (optional)

1   egg

1/4   cup chopped onion

1   (8-ounce) can cream-style corn

2   tablespoons buttermilk

In a deep fat fryer or saucepan, heat the oil (2 to 3 inches) to 375 degrees. Preheat the oven to 175 degrees. Mix the cornmeal, flour, sugar, baking powder, salt, and cayenne. Stir in the egg, onion, corn, and buttermilk until mixed. Drop the batter by the tablespoonful into the hot oil. Fry a few hush puppies at a time, turning over one or two times, until a deep golden brown, about 4 to 5 minutes. Drain on paper towels. Keep warm in the oven.

MAKES 4 TO 6 SERVINGS.

Tennessee Hush Puppies

Pearl Scarbrough
Murfreesboro, Tennessee

1/2   cup flour

1   cup cornmeal

1/4   tablespoon garlic salt

1   tablespoon sugar

1   egg

1   onion, chopped

Buttermilk

Oil for frying

Blend the flour, cornmeal, garlic salt, sugar, egg, onion, and buttermilk. Form balls, and cook in the hot oil.

MAKES 8 TO 10 SERVINGS.

Jalapeño Hush Puppies

Audrey Baxter
Grady, Alabama

1½ cups cornmeal

½ cup flour

2½ tablespoons baking powder

1½ tablespoons salt

½ tablespoon pepper

⅓ cup finely chopped onion

1 cup milk

1 egg, beaten

3 tablespoons oil

¼ cup finely chopped jalapeño peppers

Oil for frying

Combine the cornmeal, flour, baking powder, salt, pepper, onion, milk, egg, oil, and peppers. Stir until blended. Using a spoon or fork, drop into deep, hot oil. Dip the spoon or fork into hot oil each time, and the batter will drop off more easily. Fry until golden, turning once during cooking. Drain.

MAKES 8 TO 10 SERVINGS.

— BREADS —

Hoecakes

Pearl Scarbrough
Murfreesboro, Tennessee

4 cups cornmeal

1 onion, chopped

Buttermilk, about 1 pint

Corn oil for frying

Mix in a bowl the cornmeal, onion, and enough buttermilk to make a batter. Using a large skillet, heat a small amount of oil, and dip out the batter to make 4 cakes at a time. Fry until one side is brown; then turn over and cook the other side. Serve hot.

MAKES 20 TO 24 SERVINGS.

Squash Fritters

Buster and June Ducan
Manchester, Tennessee

2   cups grated yellow or white squash

2   tablespoons grated onion

Dash of pepper

2   tablespoons sugar

1   tablespoon salt

6   tablespoons flour

1   green pepper, grated (optional)

2   eggs

2   tablespoons melted butter

Combine the squash, onion, pepper, sugar, salt, flour, and green pepper, if desired. Beat the eggs, and add to the squash. Add butter. Drop by the tablespoonful on an oiled griddle. Cook as you would pancakes.

MAKES 6 TO 8 SERVINGS.

Southern Corn Bread

1   cup yellow cornmeal

¾   teaspoon salt

1   cup flour

4   teaspoons baking powder

1   medium egg, slightly beaten

1   cup skim milk

Preheat the oven to 425 degrees. Mix the cornmeal, salt, flour, and baking powder. Add the egg and milk, and mix well. Pour into a 12 x 8-inch pan sprayed with nonstick spray. Bake in the oven for 25 minutes. Cut into 12 squares.

MAKES 12 SERVINGS.

Bubba's Corn Bread

John "Bubba" Woodfin
Murfreesboro, Tennessee

5 eggs

2 (16-ounce) cans cream-style corn

1 pint sour cream

½ cup brown sugar

1 cup white sugar

1 teaspoon salt

1 cup grated cheddar cheese

Splash of cooking oil

4 cups all-purpose flour

Preheat the oven to 375 degrees. Mix well the eggs, corn, sour cream, brown sugar, white sugar, salt, cheese, cooking oil, and flour, and pour into a 9 x 13-inch pan sprayed with nonstick cooking oil. Bake in the oven for 25 to 30 minutes, until brown and done throughout. Cut into squares.

MAKES 15 TO 20 SERVINGS.

Thunderbird Corn Bread

Russell H. Pitchford
Old Hickory, Tennessee

1½ cups yellow cornmeal

½ cup all-purpose flour

3 eggs

1 cup draft beer

1 cup sour cream

¼ cup corn oil or bacon drippings

2 tablespoons baking powder

½ tablespoon salt

½ cup sugar (optional)

Preheat the oven to 425 degrees. Mix the cornmeal, flour, eggs, beer, sour cream, corn oil or bacon drippings, baking powder, salt, and sugar. Bake in a 9 x 9-inch greased pan for 25 minutes, and in the last 2 or 3 minutes turn the oven on high broil to give a thick, crisp, brown crust.

MAKES 8 TO 10 SERVINGS.

Irish Soda Bread

Annie Collier
Grady, Alabama

2   cups all-purpose flour

½ teaspoon baking powder

1   teaspoon baking soda

1   teaspoon salt

1   cup buttermilk

1   cup raisins

Preheat the oven to 350 degrees. Combine the flour, baking powder, baking soda, and salt in a medium bowl. Combine the buttermilk and raisins. Add to the flour mixture, stirring until moistened. Turn the dough onto a well-floured surface, and handle as little as possible to make dough smooth and elastic. Place on a greased baking sheet, and flatten the dough into a 1½-inch-thick circle. Bake in the oven for 30 minutes.

MAKES 1 LOAF.

Beer Bread

3   cups all-purpose flour

3¾ teaspoons baking powder

2¼ teaspoons salt

12   ounces beer

1   tablespoon honey

Grease a 9 x 5 x 3-inch loaf pan. Preheat the oven to 350 degrees. Combine the flour, baking powder, salt, beer, and honey in a large bowl. Stir until well mixed. Spread the batter in the prepared pan. Bake in the oven for 45 minutes. Turn out on a rack to cool before slicing.

MAKES 8 SERVINGS.

Banana Bread

Delsie Taylor
Cave City, Kentucky

1	cup sugar
2	eggs
½	cup butter or margarine
3	bananas, mashed
2	cups all-purpose flour
	Salt
1	tablespoon baking soda
2	tablespoons buttermilk
½	cup finely chopped nuts

Preheat the oven to 325 degrees. Mix the sugar, eggs, butter or margarine, bananas, flour, salt, baking soda, buttermilk, and nuts. Bake in a loaf pan in the oven for 50 minutes. Cool and serve.

MAKES ABOUT 10 THICK SLICES.

Cheese Onion Bread

1¼	cups water
4¼	cups bread flour
1	cup shredded cheddar cheese
¼	cup sugar
1	tablespoon minced onion
1½	teaspoons salt
1½	teaspoons yeast

Place the water, bread flour, cheddar cheese, sugar, onion, salt, and yeast in the bread machine. Select the basic/white cycle. Select the medium or light crust color, and do not use delay cycles.

MAKES A 2-POUND LOAF.

Note:

This recipe is not recommended for cast aluminum pans in a horizontal loaf shape because of inconsistent results.

Potato Tarragon Bread

Annie Collier
Grady, Alabama

1   cup water
3   tablespoons butter or
     margarine
1   egg
3   cups bread flour
³/₄   cup dry mashed
     potato mix
1   tablespoon sugar
1¹/₂ teaspoons salt
1¹/₂ teaspoons dried tarragon
     leaves
2¹/₂ teaspoons yeast

Place the water, butter or margarine, egg, bread flour, potato mix, sugar, salt, tarragon, and yeast, in that order, in a bread machine. Select the basic/white cycle. Use the medium or light crust color. Do not use the delay cycle. Remove the bread from the pan, and cool on a wire rack.

MAKES A 1¹/₂-POUND LOAF.

Sweet Potato Rolls

Annie Collier
Grady, Alabama

1   cup mashed sweet potatoes
3   tablespoons low-fat
     margarine, melted
1   package rapid rise yeast
1¹/₄ cups warm water (110 to115
     degrees)
1   large egg
1   teaspoon light salt
3   tablespoons sugar
5   cups all-purpose flour

Blend the potatoes with melted margarine. Dissolve the yeast in ¹/₂ cup warm water. Combine the potatoes with the egg, salt, sugar, and yeast mixture. Add flour alternately with remaining ³/₄ cup water, mixing until well combined. Turn onto a well-floured board and knead. Place in a bowl coated with nonstick spray. Cover and allow to rise 1 hour in a warm place. Divide the dough into 24 pieces, and form into rolls. Place on a baking sheet coated with nonstick spray, and let rise in a warm place for 30 minutes or until doubled in size. Preheat the oven to 425 degrees. Bake in the oven until done, 20 to 30 minutes.

MAKES 24 SERVINGS.

Sweet Rosemary Rolls

Mrs. Carolyn Smith
Nashville, Tennessee

1   package active dry yeast

¼   cup honey

1½ cups warm water

2   teaspoons olive oil

1   teaspoon salt

1   (6-inch) sprig fresh
    rosemary, finely chopped, or
    2 tablespoons dried

1½ cups whole wheat flour

2 to 3 cups unbleached white
    flour

    Cornmeal

    Glaze (recipe follows)

Combine the yeast, honey, and water in a medium mixing bowl. Cover and set in a warm place for 10 minutes, or until foamy. Add the oil, salt, rosemary, and whole wheat flour, and mix well. Stir in the white flour ½ cup at a time, until a stiff dough forms. Turn out the dough onto a floured surface, and knead for 5 minutes, adding flour as necessary, until the dough is smooth and elastic. Place in a lightly oiled bowl, cover with plastic wrap or a towel, and set in a warm place until doubled, about 1 hour. Dust a baking sheet with cornmeal. Punch down the dough, and divide it into 8 pieces. Form the pieces into balls, and place on prepared sheet. Cover and let rise for 30 minutes. Preheat the oven to 400 degrees. Brush the rolls lightly with the glaze, and bake in the oven for 15 to 20 minutes, until golden brown.

MAKES 8 SERVINGS.

Glaze

1   tablespoon honey

1   tablespoon warm water

Combine the honey with the water in a cup or small bowl, and stir until homogeneous.

— STUFFING —

Collier Classic Bread Stuffing

Annie Collier
Grady, Alabama

½ cup (1 stick) unsalted butter

2 medium onions, chopped

3 medium celery ribs, chopped

½ cup chopped celery leaves (from inner ribs)

1 pound ½-inch cubes white bread, dried, or 10 cups plain bread croutons

¼ cup chopped fresh parsley

2 teaspoons poultry seasoning

1½ teaspoons salt

½ teaspoon freshly ground pepper

1½ to 2 cups turkey or chicken broth, as needed

In a large skillet, melt the butter over medium heat. Add the onions, celery, and celery leaves. Cook, stirring often, until the onions are golden, about 8 minutes. Scrape the vegetables and butter into a large bowl. Mix in the bread cubes or croutons, parsley, poultry seasoning, salt, and pepper. Gradually stir in about 1½ cups broth, until the stuffing is evenly moistened but not soggy. Use the mixture as a stuffing or place in a lightly buttered casserole, drizzle with ½ cup broth, cover, and bake for 30 to 40 minutes.

MAKES 8 TO 10 SERVINGS.

Duck decoys should be tied with dark-colored anchor lines so they aren't visible to the ducks overhead.

Wild Turkey Stuffing

Wild turkey gizzard, liver, and heart

1 large loaf sliced bread

½ celery rib, sliced

2 large white onions, peeled

¼ cup butter

2 ½ tablespoons lard

2 cups chopped pecans

Salt and pepper

Boil the gizzard, liver, and heart in water until very tender. Cut all the gristle off the gizzard. Save the broth. Toast each slice of bread well on both sides. Grind separately the toasted bread, celery, onions, and turkey giblets, and reserve in separate dishes. In a large frying pan sauté the onions in butter and lard. Add the celery and giblets. Sprinkle in the toast crumbs and pecans. Salt and pepper to taste. Add just enough broth to make a lightly moist stuffing.

MAKES 12 TO 15 SERVINGS, OR ENOUGH STUFFING TO STUFF A 12- TO 15-POUND TURKEY.

Sausage-Pecan Stuffing

Annie Collier
Grady, Alabama

1 cup chopped celery

¾ to 1 cup chopped onion

½ cup bell pepper

1 stick margarine

8 cups crumbled corn bread

5 cups toasted white bread, cubed, or 3 cups bread crumbs

5 cups canned chicken broth

½ pound pork sausage

Giblets from wild turkey or chicken, finely chopped (optional)

½ teaspoon salt

¼ tablespoon black pepper

4 eggs, slightly beaten

1 cup chopped pecans

In a heavy skillet, cook the celery, onion, and bell pepper in margarine until tender. Place the corn bread and cubes or crumbs in a large bowl, and add heated chicken broth and sautéed vegetables, mixing well. Cook the sausage until browned, adding giblets when almost done. Add to the bread mixture the seasonings, eggs, and chopped pecans. Toss lightly to mix well. Preheat the oven to 325 degrees. Put the stuffing in a 13 x 9 x 2-inch pan; do not cover. Bake in the oven for 45 minutes.

MAKES 15 TO 20 SERVINGS, OR ENOUGH STUFFING FOR AN 18- TO 20-POUND WILD TURKEY.

Almond-Sausage Stuffing

Annie Collier
Grady, Alabama

1	**cup slivered almonds**
1	**pound pork sausage**
8	**cups dry bread cubes**
2	**cups thinly sliced celery**
1	**cup chopped onions**
1	**(8-ounce) can sliced mushrooms**
1	**teaspoon poultry seasoning**
½	**cup liquid from canned mushrooms**
1	**egg, slightly beaten**

To roast the almonds, place in an oiled pan on the stove, and stir frequently until golden. Brown the sausage in a skillet, breaking the sausage apart as it cooks. Drain the sausage, but reserve the drippings in the skillet. Add the sausage to the bread cubes. Add the celery, onions, and mushrooms to the drippings in the skillet. Cook until tender-crisp. Stir the vegetables into the sausage mixture along with the almonds and poultry seasoning. Heat the mushroom liquid, and pour over the stuffing. Add the egg, and toss until mixed thoroughly.

MAKES 12 SERVINGS OR ENOUGH TO STUFF A 20-POUND BIRD.

If you wait too long to charge your boat's electric motor batteries or fail to charge them for a proper amount of time, you'll be faced with replacing those batteries sooner than you'd like. Deep-cycle batteries should be charged within 24 hours of use and should be kept fully charged while stored. Check with your battery dealer or manufacturer for specific charging requirements.

Night fishing for stripers is usually better during the waxing of the new moon or the waning of the half-moon. Fish before the moon rises or after the moon sets to find alewife and stripers moving toward the bank. Nights with a bright moon will usually draw the bait and stripers to open water.

Chestnut Stuffing

Mrs. Carolyn Smith
Nashville, Tennessee

2   onions, chopped

4   ribs celery, chopped

3   tablespoons fresh parsley

1   teaspoon poultry seasoning

¼   teaspoon pepper seasoning

2   tablespoons light margarine

3   cups canned peeled chestnuts, drained and coarsely chopped

6   cups bread cubes

½   cup saltine cracker crumbs

1   cup raisins

1   cup apple juice

¼   cup skim milk

¼   cup fat-free egg substitute

In a nonstick skillet over medium-high heat, sauté the onions, celery, parsley, poultry seasoning, and pepper in the margarine until the vegetables are tender, 4 to 5 minutes. Remove from the heat. Mix the vegetables, chestnuts, bread cubes, crackers, raisins, apple juice, milk, and egg substitute in a bowl. Preheat the oven to 325 degrees. Coat a 9 x 13-inch baking pan with nonstick spray. Spoon the stuffing into a pan, and cover with foil. Bake in the oven until heated through, about 45 minutes.

MAKES 8 SERVINGS.

Wild Turkey Stuffing with Beef and Sausage

Kay Whitsett

1 **pound white bread, cut in small pieces**

1½ **cups chicken stock**

1 **tablespoon vermouth or sherry**

1½ **teaspoons powdered sage**

½ **teaspoon dried rosemary**

2 **garlic cloves, crushed**

3 **slices bacon, cut in pieces**

4 **tablespoons butter**

1 **cup chopped onions**

½ **cup chopped celery**

¼ **cup fresh parsley**

½ **pound ground chuck**

½ **pound pork sausage**

1½ **teaspoons salt**

¼ **teaspoon pepper**

In a large bowl, combine the bread crumbs and chicken stock. In a saucepan over low heat, warm the vermouth, and add the sage, rosemary, and garlic. Mix well and set aside. Fry the bacon until crisp in a skillet over medium heat; remove it with a slotted spoon, and add it to the bread mixture. In the same skillet, melt the butter with the bacon drippings. Add the onions, celery, and parsley. Cook over medium heat until the vegetables are tender, about 10 minutes. Then add the ground chuck and pork sausage, and cook until done. Add the meat and vegetable mixture to the bread mixture. Pour the reserved spice mixture over the stuffing, and season with salt and pepper. Mix thoroughly until well blended. Taste and correct seasonings, if necessary.

MAKES ABOUT 10 CUPS, ENOUGH FOR A 12-POUND BIRD.

Turkey hunters have figured out that shiny guns and sharp-eyed gobblers don't mix. Deer hunters have been slower to learn this. It doesn't matter how well you are camouflaged if you are waving around a bright, reflective gun.

If you have trouble removing pork chunks from your jigs, push one end of a coffee stirrer straw over the hook barb, and the pork will slide right off.

Corn Bread–Sausage Stuffing

Annie Collier
Grady, Alabama

1   recipe corn bread, made from a mix

¾   pound turkey sausage with casings removed

1   tablespoon light margarine

2   cups chopped onions

1½ cups chopped celery

2   teaspoons dried sage

1   teaspoon dried marjoram

1   teaspoon dried rosemary, crumbled

½   cup nonalcoholic white wine

½   cup sliced green onions

¼   cup fat-free egg substitute

1   cup reduced-fat chicken broth

Preheat the oven to 375 degrees. Crumble the corn bread into a large, shallow pan. Bake in the oven, stirring often, until crumbs are golden brown, 15 to 20 minutes. Break up the sausage, and cook over medium-high heat in a nonstick skillet until browned and cooked through, 5 to 7 minutes. Transfer to a bowl. Reduce oven temperature to 325 degrees. Add the margarine to the skillet, and heat until melted. Add the onions and celery. Cook, stirring often, until vegetables are tender, 4 to 5 minutes. Add the sage, marjoram, and rosemary. Cook, stirring constantly for 2 minutes. Add the vegetable mixture to the sausage. Mix in the corn bread, wine, onions, and egg substitute. Coat a 3-quart casserole with nonstick spray. Spoon the stuffing into the casserole, and drizzle with the broth. Cover and bake at 325 degrees for 30 minutes. Uncover to bake until golden, 20 to 30 minutes.

MAKES 8 SERVINGS.

Apple-Raisin Whole Wheat Stuffing

12 cups cubed whole wheat bread

1½ cups raisins

4 apples (not peeled), chopped

1½ cups finely chopped onion

4 cups thinly sliced celery

3 eggs (or egg whites)

1 cup chopped walnuts or pecans

4 tablespoons melted margarine

2½ cups chicken broth

½ teaspoon freshly ground black pepper

If the bread is not stale, spread the slices out on a rack or counter for half a day to dry and then cut into cubes. Combine the bread cubes with raisins, apples, onion, celery, eggs, walnuts or pecans, margarine, chicken broth, and black pepper. Stuff the turkey or bake in a covered oven-proof dish for about 40 minutes at 325 degrees (or whatever temperature you are using for your turkey).

MAKES 12 SERVINGS.

Note:

An alternate cooking method is to spoon the stuffing into a Crock-Pot and cook on high for 2 hours; then cook on low for 4 hours.

When hunting snow geese, the more calls you have the better. Try using two electronic calls plus your mouth call.

Chapter 10

Side Dishes

Salads, Vegetables, Fruit, Grits, Rice, Beans

Not only do viewers send me their favorite fish and game recipes—they also send me recipes for side dishes that complement them. Combine the recipes in this chapter with your favorite fish and game recipes, and you'll have a spectacular meal.

— SALADS —

Granny's Slaw

Bill Flenn

1   medium head cabbage, shredded

2   tablespoons chopped fresh parsley

1   cup shredded carrots

1   cup finely chopped green pepper

¼   cup chopped green onion

3   tablespoons vinegar

1   cup mayonnaise

1   tablespoon mustard

Dash of garlic powder

Salt and pepper

Dash of cayenne

Combine the cabbage, parsley, carrots, green pepper, and onion in a large bowl. Whisk together the vinegar, mayonnaise, mustard, garlic powder, salt, pepper, and cayenne in a smaller bowl, and pour over the cabbage mixture, stirring and coating well. Cover and refrigerate 2 to 3 hours before serving. Stir again before serving.

MAKES 6 TO 8 SERVINGS.

Cheddar Potato Salad

12 cups diced, cooked potatoes

2 cups sliced celery

8 hard-cooked eggs, chopped

4 cups (1 pound) shredded, sharp cheddar cheese

¾ cup sliced green onions

2 cups salad dressing

1 tablespoon prepared mustard

1 tablespoon salt

¼ teaspoon pepper

Combine the potatoes, celery, eggs, cheese, and onion, and lightly mix. In a separate bowl, combine the salad dressing, mustard, and seasonings, and mix lightly. Pour the dressing over the potato mixture and mix gently. Chill.

MAKES 20 TO 22 SERVINGS.

Dutch Potato Salad

6 ounces mild cheddar or Monterey Jack cheese

2½ pounds red potatoes

5 slices bacon, cooked and crumbled

½ cup sliced green onions

1½ cups mayonnaise

½ cup light cream

¼ cup mustard

½ teaspoon pepper

Julienne the cheese into 1-inch pieces. In a covered pan, cook the potatoes in boiling water for 20 to 25 minutes, or until just tender, and drain. Peel and cut the potatoes into ½-inch cubes. In a very large bowl, combine the potatoes, bacon, cheese, and onions. In a separate medium bowl, combine the mayonnaise, cream, mustard, and pepper; add to the potatoes. Toss to coat. Cover and chill for 6 to 24 hours.

MAKES 10 SERVINGS.

— VEGETABLES —

Cranberry Beets

1   cup water

1   cup sugar

2   cups raw cranberries

1   teaspoon cornstarch

1   tablespoon cold water

1   (16-ounce) can cubed beets

Mix the water and sugar, and boil for 5 minutes. Add the washed cranberries, and cook without stirring until the cranberries pop open, about 5 minutes. Drain the juice from the cranberries, and return the juice to the heat. Mix the cornstarch with the cold water to make a smooth paste. Add to the juice, and cook until clear and thickened, about 3 to 4 minutes. Add the berries and the drained beets to the thickened juice. Heat all together until hot. If you use whole or sliced beets, cut them into cubes. Serve hot or cold.

MAKES 8 SERVINGS.

Tallman Cabbage

Ronnie "Tallman" Polson
Nashville, Tennessee

1   large head cabbage, chopped

1   large onion, chopped

1   large green pepper, chopped

2   pounds sausage

1   (16-ounce) can tomato sauce

Boil the chopped cabbage in a large pot with 2 to 3 inches of water. Add the onion and pepper. Brown the sausage, and add to the cabbage. Add the tomato sauce, and "let simmer 'til your lips start smackin'."

MAKES 4 TO 6 SERVINGS.

Cabbage Rolls with Sour Cream Sauce

1	pound ground turkey sausage
½	cup diced onions
½	cup diced celery
1	cup cooked rice
1	teaspoon prepared horseradish
1	teaspoon prepared brown mustard
¼	cup fat-free egg substitute
8	large cabbage leaves
¼	cup tomato sauce
½	cup water
1	cup nonfat sour cream

Coat a large skillet with nonstick spray. Warm over low heat, and sauté the sausage and onions until lightly browned. Remove from the heat, and add the celery, rice, horseradish, mustard, and egg substitute. Fill a 3-quart saucepan with water, and bring it to a boil. Add the cabbage, and cook for 3 minutes. Drain the cabbage in a colander. Divide the meat mixture among the cabbage leaves. Roll up the leaves, and fasten with toothpicks. Preheat the oven to 350 degrees. Coat a 7 x 11-inch baking dish with nonstick spray, and add the rolled cabbage leaves. Pour the tomato sauce mixed with the ½ cup water over the rolls. Cover and bake in the oven for 30 minutes. Using a slotted spoon, transfer the cabbage rolls to a platter. Add the sour cream to the liquid in the baking dish, and whisk to combine. Serve over the cabbage rolls.

MAKES 8 SERVINGS.

Cauliflower Parmesan

1	cauliflower head, separated into 12 florets
1	tablespoon salt
½	cup bread crumbs
½	cup grated Parmesan cheese
1	egg
1	tablespoon milk
2	tablespoons melted margarine

Cook the cauliflower for 7 minutes in salted water. Drain. Mix the bread crumbs with the cheese. Beat the egg with the milk. Dip each floret in the egg wash, then in the crumb mixture. Preheat the oven to 350 degrees. Arrange the cauliflower in a buttered casserole. Pour the melted margarine over the cauliflower. Cover and bake in the oven for 20 minutes.

MAKES 6 SERVINGS.

Summer Corn

4 ears sweet corn

2 yellow squash, sliced

1 medium onion, chopped

Salt and pepper

1 tablespoon water (optional)

¼ cup butter

In a large bowl, cut the corn from the cob, scraping the cob to get the milk. Add the squash, onion, salt, and pepper. If the mixture seems dry, add the water, 1 tablespoon at a time, to moisten. You will want some liquid to form in the bottom of the bowl. Melt the butter in a large skillet. Add the corn mixture. Cook, covered, over medium heat until squash and onions are tender, about 10 to 15 minutes. Stir occasionally. Uncover, increase the heat to medium-high, and stir frequently until lightly browned. If the mixture appears sticky, you can add more butter or water. Serve immediately.

MAKES 4 SERVINGS.

Azure Eggplant

5 small eggplants, peeled and cut into small cubes

Salted water

1 medium onion, chopped

1 medium bell pepper, chopped

2 tablespoons butter

2 to 3 tablespoons cooking oil

1¼ pounds ground beef

2 cups cooked rice

Salt and pepper

Bread crumbs

Butter

Soak the eggplants in salted water for 20 minutes. Drain. Sauté the onion, bell pepper, and eggplant in butter and oil until tender and wilted. Add ground beef, and cook until the meat is no longer red. Add the cooked rice, salt, and pepper. Cook until the rice is hot and blended with other ingredients. Preheat the oven to 325 degrees. Place the eggplant mixture in a casserole, sprinkle lightly with the bread crumbs, and dot with the butter. Bake uncovered in the oven for 20 minutes.

MAKES 6 TO 8 SERVINGS.

Italian Green Beans and Tomatoes

¾ **pound green beans**

½ **cup red onion rings**

¼ **cup Italian dressing**

2 **tomatoes, cut into thin wedges**

2 **tablespoons chopped fresh basil**

Place the green beans, onion, and dressing in a microwavable bowl and cover. Microwave on high 8 to 10 minutes, or until the beans are crisp-tender, stirring after 2 minutes. Stir in the tomatoes and basil.

MAKES 6 SERVINGS.

Spiked Sautéed Mushrooms

1 **tablespoon butter**

4 **cups whole mushrooms**

½ **cup chopped onion**

1 **teaspoon garlic salt**

¼ **cup chicken broth**

½ **cup beef broth**

1 **cup Chablis wine**

Heat the butter in a skillet until melted. Add the mushrooms and onions, and cook until onions are tender. Add the garlic salt, both broths, and wine. Simmer 15 minutes. Serve over game.

MAKES 8 SERVINGS.

Buttermilk Batter Onion Rings

1 **large onion (about a pound)**

1 **cup buttermilk pancake mix**

1 **cup buttermilk**

1 **egg**

Vegetable oil

Cut the onion into one-inch slices, and separate into rings. Spread the pancake mix on waxed paper, or place in a paper bag. In a medium bowl, beat the buttermilk and egg with a fork until smooth. Dip a few onion rings at a time into the buttermilk mixture, and then coat thoroughly with the pancake mix. Put the onion rings on a rack until dry, 1½ to 2 hours. In a deep fat fryer or saucepan, heat the oil (2 to 3 inches deep) to 375 degrees. Fry a few rings at a time, turning over one or two times until golden brown, 1 to 2 minutes. Drain on paper towels.

MAKES 4 TO 6 SERVINGS.

Comforting Creamy Potatoes

2 **pounds Russet potatoes**

3 **garlic cloves, minced**

2 **cups chicken stock**

1/4 **teaspoon white pepper**

Salt

1/2 **cup heavy cream**

Chopped chives

Peel the potatoes, and cut into 1/2-inch cubes. Place the potatoes in a heavy saucepan. Stir in the garlic, chicken stock, pepper, and salt. Bring the mixture to a boil and stir. Reduce the heat to very low, cover, and simmer for 10 minutes, stirring occasionally. The potatoes are cooked when they are soft at the edges but still retain their shape. The broth should be creamy and thick. If not, stir the potatoes to give off more starch. Just before serving, stir the cream into the hot potato mixture. Heat briefly, just enough to warm. If desired, add more cream. You should end up with soft cubes of potatoes in a creamy, rich sauce. Garnish with a sprinkling of chives before serving.

MAKES 4 TO 6 SERVINGS.

Rosemary Garlic New Potatoes

1 **large sprig fresh rosemary**

12 **ounces new potatoes**

1 **tablespoon minced garlic in oil**

1/2 **teaspoon salt**

1/2 **teaspoon pepper**

2 **tablespoons water**

Preheat the oven to 375 degrees. Mix the rosemary, potatoes, garlic in oil, salt, pepper, and water in a medium-size baking dish. Cover and bake in the oven for 30 minutes or until tender.

MAKES 4 SERVINGS.

Potato and Onion Pie

2 tablespoons butter

1 cup new potato slices,
   ⅛ inch thick

1 medium onion, thinly sliced
   and separated into rings

⅓ cup chopped parsley

⅓ cup milk

8 eggs, beaten

1 cup shredded Swiss cheese

½ teaspoon salt

¼ teaspoon pepper

1 medium ripe tomato, cut in
   ¼-inch slices

Preheat the oven to 400 degrees. In a 10-inch, ovenproof skillet, melt the butter in the oven for about 3 to 4 minutes. Add the potatoes and onion. Bake for 15 to 20 minutes, until crisp-tender, stirring once. In a large bowl, stir together the parsley, milk, eggs, Swiss cheese, salt, and pepper. Pour the mixture over the potatoes and onion, and arrange tomato slices over the top. Return to the oven, and continue to bake for 17 to 22 minutes until the eggs are set and lightly browned.

MAKES 4 SERVINGS.

One or two seconds after shooting a buck with your bow, blow your grunt. Often the deer will hear the call and lie down to die.

Garlic Mashed Potatoes

1 envelope roasted garlic salad
   dressing mix

6 cups hot mashed
   potatoes

Stir the salad dressing mix into the hot potatoes. Serve immediately.

MAKES 6 SERVINGS.

Hot Deviled Potatoes

2 cups mashed potatoes

½ cup nonfat sour cream or yogurt

2 teaspoons prepared mustard

½ teaspoon salt

½ teaspoon sugar

2 tablespoons chopped green onion

Paprika

Prepare the potatoes (if instant, according to package directions), or warm leftover potatoes. Heat the sour cream in a medium saucepan, being careful not to boil. Add the mustard, salt, and sugar, and blend. Stir the sour cream mixture into the hot potatoes. Add onion and blend. Spoon into foil baking shells, and sprinkle with the paprika.

MAKES 4 SERVINGS.

Broiled Tomatoes

4 medium ripe tomatoes

¼ cup cracker crumbs

½ teaspoon salt

½ teaspoon dried oregano or basil

½ teaspoon dried thyme

1 tablespoon oil

Preheat the oven to broil. Wash the tomatoes, and slice in half crosswise. Place on a baking sheet, cut side up. Mix the crumbs, seasonings, and oil. Sprinkle some of the mixture on each tomato. Broil 8 to 10 inches from the heat, about 4 minutes, or until golden brown. Garnish with parsley sprigs.

MAKES 4 SERVINGS.

Unlike other waterfowl, wood ducks almost always seek a tree cavity. The nesting tree will usually border a stream or lake, but woodies may nest a mile or more from water.

Jimmy's Tomato Pie

1 (9-inch) piecrust, unbaked

2 to 4 tomatoes

   Seasoning salt

$\frac{1}{2}$ teaspoon basil

$\frac{1}{8}$ cup chopped fresh chives

$\frac{1}{4}$ cup mayonnaise

1 cup cheddar cheese

Preheat the oven to 425 degrees, and cook the piecrust for 5 minutes. Cut the tomatoes in thick slices to cover the bottom of the pie crust, and sprinkle with the seasoning salt. Sprinkle the basil and chives over the tomatoes. Mix the mayonnaise with the cheese, and spread over the top to seal the tomatoes. Reduce oven temperature to 400 degrees. Put the pie in the oven, and bake for 30 to 35 minutes.

MAKES 8 SERVINGS.

Stuffed Squash

2 yellow crookneck squash, sliced in half lengthwise

8 strips bacon, cooked and crumbled

$\frac{1}{3}$ cup bread crumbs

$\frac{1}{3}$ cup sour cream

   Seasoned salt

   Pepper

4 slices Swiss cheese

Place the squash cut side down in a microwavable dish. Microwave on high for 3 minutes, turning after $1\frac{1}{2}$ minutes. Check to make sure the seeded part of the squash is mushy. After the squash has cooled slightly, scoop out the fleshy part, reserving the shells, and mix the squash with the bacon, bread crumbs, sour cream, salt, and pepper. Put the mixture back into the squash boats, and top with Swiss cheese. Put under the broiler until the cheese has browned.

MAKES 4 SERVINGS.

 If panfish (bluegill) are coming slow on popping bugs, tie a 12- to 16-inch piece of 2- or 4-pound test line to the eye of the poppers and attach a small trout nymph or dark-colored wet fly to the leader. The surface bug will attract the quarry and act as a strike indicator; many of the fish will nail the nymph or wet fly dangling below.

Crystal Ginger Sweet Potatoes

4   medium-size sweet potatoes

3   tablespoons butter

⅓   cup crystallized ginger, cut into small pieces

½   cup orange juice

¼   cup firmly packed brown sugar

Peel and boil the sweet potatoes until tender but firm; cut into slices. Preheat the oven to 375 degrees. Arrange a layer of the sliced potatoes in a buttered casserole. Dot with the butter, and sprinkle with the ginger. Repeat with the next layer. Pour the orange juice over the potatoes, and sprinkle with the brown sugar. Bake uncovered in the oven for 45 minutes. Baste occasionally to keep moist.

MAKES 6 SERVINGS.

Easy Yummy Yams

4 to 5 fresh yams

Unsweetened apple juice

Butter or margarine (optional)

Cinnamon (optional)

Cloves (optional)

Nutmeg (optional)

1   (6-ounce) can apple juice concentrate

Peel, wash, and cut the yams in chunks, and put in a large pan. Cover the yams with the apple juice, and bring to a boil. Cook until tender. Mash the yams, blending in the butter, cinnamon, cloves, nutmeg, and apple juice concentrate to the desired consistency.

MAKES 4 TO 6 SERVINGS.

— FRUIT —

Poached Apples

5   cooking apples

1   cup sugar

2   cups water

1/4 teaspoon salt

5 to 6 drops red food coloring

1/2 teaspoon cinnamon extract

1/4 teaspoon nutmeg extract

1   teaspoon vanilla

Pare the apples, and cut them in half crosswise. Pick out the seeds, but do not core. Combine the sugar, water, salt, food coloring, cinnamon extract, nutmeg extract, and vanilla in a large skillet, and bring to a boil to make a syrup. Stir in the apples, and simmer until tender, watching carefully, so they will not get too tender all at once.

MAKES 10 SERVINGS.

Note:

If nutmeg and cinnamon flavoring extracts are not obtainable, use the same amounts of the dry spice, mixing with the 1 cup sugar before adding to the water.

Minted Apple Rings

1   cup sugar

2³/₄ cups water

1/8 teaspoon green food coloring

2   tart, medium-size apples (not peeled)

2   teaspoons mint flavoring

Mix the sugar, water, and food coloring in a heavy skillet. Boil for 5 minutes to form a syrup. Slice the apples crosswise about 1/4-inch thick. Do not core the apples, but remove the seeds. Add the mint flavoring to the syrup, and place the apple slices in the syrup. Boil over medium heat for 15 to 20 minutes, or until the apples become transparent. Turn the slices occasionally, and baste with the syrup. Remove the slices from the syrup and cool.

MAKES 2 TO 4 SERVINGS.

Fresh Applesauce

¼ cup water

2 tablespoons lemon juice

¼ cup sugar

4 medium apples

Place the water, lemon juice, and sugar in a blender or food processor. Wash, core, and cut up the apples; put in the blender or processor. Blend until well processed. Serve immediately.

MAKES 3 SERVINGS.

Heavy jigs are needed in strong winds or when you're fishing in current or deep water. The key is to maintain bottom contact. Keep asking, "Am I touching bottom?"

Scalloped Pineapple

Debbie White

This is good served warm with whipped cream; the taste is very much like a pineapple upside-down cake. —DEBBIE WHITE

2 cups sugar

2 sticks margarine

3 eggs, beaten

1 (16-ounce) can crushed pineapple

4 cups white bread crumbs

Preheat the oven to 350 degrees. Cream the sugar and margarine together; add the eggs and mix well. Add the pineapple to the mixture, then the bread crumbs, and stir well. Bake in an ovenproof dish for 1¼ hours.

MAKES 12 SERVINGS.

Curried Baked Fruit

Brenda Nance
Nashville, Tennessee

1   **(24-ounce) can pear halves**

1   **(20-ounce) can pineapple chunks**

1   **(24-ounce) can peach halves**

¼   **cup sliced maraschino cherries**

⅓   **cup butter or margarine**

2   **teaspoons curry powder**

¾   **cup light brown sugar**

Preheat the oven to 325 degrees. Drain the pear halves, pineapple chunks, peach halves, and maraschino cherries, and place in a casserole dish. Melt the butter in a saucepan, and add the curry powder and sugar. Mix well. Pour over the fruit, and bake uncovered in the oven for 1 hour. Serve with wild game.

MAKES 6 TO 8 SERVINGS.

— GRITS, RICE, AND BEANS —

Some of the recipes in this section, such as the chilis, could actually be meals in themselves. They're perfect for hungry outdoorsmen.

Jimmy's Jambalaya Grits

2   **tablespoons bacon grease**

2   **tablespoons flour**

½   **cup chopped onion**

1   **green pepper, chopped**

½   **cup chopped celery**

1   **cup quick grits, uncooked**

1   **cup peeled and chopped fresh tomatoes**

1   **cup ground ham**

    Cooked bacon

In a heavy skillet, heat the bacon grease, and gradually add the flour, stirring constantly until the roux is light brown. Add the onion, green pepper, and celery, and cook 5 minutes. Cook the grits according to the package directions, and add to the roux, breaking up the grits if necessary. Add the tomatoes and ham. Sprinkle with the bacon and serve immediately.

MAKES 6 TO 8 SERVINGS.

Browned Butter Rice

¼ cup margarine

1 cup quick-cooking rice

1 cup chicken stock, or 1 chicken bouillon cube mixed with 1 cup boiling water

Salt

Brown the margarine in a skillet. Add the rice, and stir until all grains are coated with the margarine. Slowly add the chicken stock. Season with salt and stir. Cover and simmer rice for 20 minutes.

MAKES 4 SERVINGS.

Rice Casserole

1 cup rice

4 teaspoons melted margarine

2 cups chicken broth

¾ cup slivered almonds

¾ cup chopped parsley

¾ cup chopped green onions

¾ cup chopped carrots

¾ cup chopped celery

Preheat the oven to 350 degrees. Coat the rice with melted margarine. Place in a casserole and add the chicken broth. Bake uncovered for 40 minutes. Stir in the almonds, parsley, green onions, carrots, and celery. Cook 15 minutes longer.

MAKES 4 SERVINGS.

The embellished Carolina rig uses a three-way swivel in place of the normal two-way. Rig your leader as you normally would. On the third swivel connection, place a leader about one-third to one-half as long as the other leader, and use a smaller plastic bait, such as a floating 4-inch worm or grub on that hook.

Curried Rice

1   tablespoon minced onion

2   tablespoons butter or
     margarine

1/2 to 1 teaspoon curry powder

1/4 teaspoon salt

1/4 teaspoon pepper

3   cups hot, cooked rice

1/4 cup slivered almonds,
     toasted

1/4 cup chopped pimiento-
     stuffed olives or pitted ripe
     olives

In a small skillet, cook and stir the onion in the butter until the onion is tender. Stir in the curry powder, salt, and pepper. Mix into the hot rice. Sprinkle the almonds and olives over the rice.

MAKES 6 SERVINGS.

Wild Rice with Leeks and Mushrooms

This dish is perfect for all types of game, meat, or fowl.   —JIMMY

3   cups water

1 1/2 cups wild rice

3 1/4 cups fat-free chicken broth

1   tablespoon olive oil

3   leeks, chopped

1/2 cup sliced mushrooms

1/4 teaspoon ground black
     pepper

In a large saucepan, combine the water and rice. Bring to a boil over high heat. Cover, remove from the heat, and let stand for 20 minutes. Drain rice well, and return to the pan. Add 3 cups of the broth. Bring to a boil over medium-high heat. Stir, cover, reduce the heat, and simmer for 25 minutes, or until the rice is just tender, and the liquid has been absorbed. While the rice is cooking, warm the oil in a large nonstick skillet over medium heat. Add the leeks, and sauté for 3 minutes. Add the mushrooms, and sauté for 3 minutes. Add the pepper and the remaining 1/4 cup broth. Cover and simmer for 5 minutes. When the rice is done, add the vegetable mixture to the rice pan, and mix well.

MAKES 8 SERVINGS.

The commonly accepted standard for chokes is based on the percentage of your shot that is placed in a 30-inch circle at 40 yards.

· Improved cylinder places 40 to 50 percent of the shot in a 30-inch circle.

· Modified choke places 55 to 65 percent in a 30-inch circle.

· Full choke places 70 to 75 percent of the shot in a 30-inch circle.

Tennessee Beans and Rice

1¼ pounds dried pinto beans

7 cups water

1 small ham hock

1 medium onion, chopped

2 cloves garlic, minced

½ teaspoon salt

1 pound ring of smoked beef and pork sausage, thickly sliced

1 (10-ounce) can tomatoes with green chilies, with juice

½ cup rice

Sort and wash the beans. Combine the beans, water, ham hock, onion, garlic, and salt in a large Dutch oven. Bring to a boil. Cover, reduce the heat to medium, and cook 45 minutes. Add the sausage, tomatoes with green chilies, and rice. Cover, reduce heat, and simmer 1 hour or until the beans are done, stirring occasionally. Remove the ham hock, shred the ham from the bone, and return the ham to the bean mixture.

MAKES 6 SERVINGS.

Red Beans and Rice

1	pound dry red beans, soaked overnight
3	quarts water
1	yellow onion, peeled and chopped
1	scallion, chopped
7	garlic cloves, peeled and minced
½	cup chopped fresh parsley
1	rib celery, chopped
½	cup catsup
1	green bell pepper, seeded and chopped
1	tablespoon Worcestershire sauce
2	teaspoons Tabasco
2	bay leaves
1	teaspoon dried thyme
1	pound smoked sausage, cut into 1-inch pieces
1	pound pickled pork, cut into 1-inch cubes
	Salt and pepper
	Cooked rice for 6 servings

Drain the red beans that have been soaked overnight. Place them in a 6-quart heavy pot, and add the fresh water. Cover, and simmer for 1 hour, or until the beans are tender. Watch the amount of water; the beans must be covered with water at all times. Add additional water to cover if necessary. Add the yellow and green onions, garlic, parsley, celery, catsup, green bell pepper, Worcestershire sauce, Tabasco, bay leaves, thyme, sausage, and pork to the pot. Adjust the seasoning with salt and pepper to taste. Simmer the mixture, partially covered, for 1 to 2 hours, or until the liquid has thickened. Serve over a bed of cooked rice.

MAKES 6 SERVINGS.

Bucks, particularly big ones, avoid open areas most of the time and are exceptionally shy about leaving cover during hunting season.

 Don't feel downhearted if your fishing hours go by without success. Experiment constantly, keeping mental notes on what types of spots you've been fishing and what presentations you've been using. Think about how much closer you are to catching your next fish as you eliminate unproductive spots and methods.

South of the Border Black Beans and Rice

1 teaspoon olive oil

½ cup chopped onion

½ cup chopped green bell pepper

3 garlic cloves, minced

2 cups cooked black beans

1 cup black bean broth or water

2 tablespoons brewed coffee

2 cups cooled cooked rice

1 teaspoon Worcestershire sauce

Salt and pepper

2 tablespoons chopped fresh cilantro

Heat the oil in a large, heavy skillet. Add the onion, bell pepper, and garlic. Cook until the onion is translucent, stirring occasionally, about 10 minutes. Add the beans, broth, and coffee. Simmer until slightly thickened, about 15 minutes. Add the rice, Worcestershire sauce, salt, and pepper. Simmer 5 minutes to blend flavors. Garnish with cilantro and serve.

MAKES 4 SERVINGS.

White Chili

2 pounds ground turkey

2 medium white onions, chopped

2 tablespoons minced garlic

2 teaspoons oregano

4 tablespoons cumin

2 (4-ounce) jars chopped green chilies

3 (7-ounce) cans green tomatillo salsa or salsa verde

3 (16-ounce) cans white beans, rinsed and drained

2 (14½-ounce) cans chicken broth

Nacho chips

Shredded cheddar cheese

Chopped green onions

Sauté the ground turkey with the onions, garlic, oregano, cumin, and chilies until browned; drain the fat. Remove mixture to a large pot. Add the salsa, beans, and chicken broth. Cook for 45 minutes to 1 hour to blend the flavors. Serve with Nacho chips, shredded cheddar cheese, and chopped green onions.

MAKES 8 SERVINGS.

Pheasant Creek Hunting Preserve Chili

This recipe is for 5 gallons. It's the only way Jesse Dunaway, owner of Pheasant Creek Hunting Preserve, knows how to make it. Jesse leaves the chili on the stove burner on low all day long, and he stirs it occasionally during that time. —JIMMY

8 pounds ground round beef

3 packages mild chili seasoning

12 (16-ounce) cans chili-hot beans

2 medium onions, chopped

6 (16-ounce) cans stewed tomatoes

2 (8-ounce) cans mushrooms

Brown the ground beef. Add the chili seasoning, beans, onions, tomatoes, and mushrooms. Cook for 30 minutes, stirring occasionally.

MAKES 25 TO 30 SERVINGS.

Southwest Baked Beans

1   **pound ground chuck**

½   **cup honey**

¼   **cup catsup**

1   **tablespoon cider vinegar**

1   **teaspoon chili powder**

1   **teaspoon salt**

1   **(32-ounce) can black beans
    or kidney beans, rinsed**

1   **(12-ounce) can whole kernel
    corn, drained**

1   **(4-ounce) can chopped
    green chilies, drained,
    or 1 large jalapeño, seeded
    and chopped**

½   **cup chopped onion**

2   **tablespoons chopped
    cilantro**

    **Red bell pepper rings for
    garnish**

    Cilantro sprigs for garnish

Preheat the oven to 350 degrees. Brown and drain the ground beef. In a 1½-quart casserole, combine the honey, catsup, vinegar, chili powder, salt, beans, corn, green chilies, onion, and cilantro. Add the browned ground chuck. Cover and bake in the oven for 45 minutes, stirring occasionally. Arrange the bell pepper rings over the top, re-cover, and continue baking 15 minutes. Garnish with the cilantro sprigs.

MAKES 6 SERVINGS.

Chapter 11

Soups

Many of the soups in this chapter are made with fish or game. Others just taste great as accompaniments to fish or game.

Fish Noodle Soup

Mrs. James Milton
Nashville, Tennessee

2	**medium carrots**
1	**quart water**
1	**celery rib**
1	**small onion, cut into thin wedges**
¼	**cup snipped fresh parsley**
2	**teaspoons instant chicken bouillon granules**
½	**teaspoon salt**
¼	**teaspoon dried thyme leaves**
⅛	**teaspoon pepper**
½	**cup uncooked narrow egg noodles**
1	**cup flaked, cooked, lean fish**

Cut the carrots into diagonal slices. Cut the celery into thin slices. In a 2-quart saucepan, combine the carrots, water, celery, onion, parsley, bouillon granules, salt, thyme, and pepper. Heat to boiling. Reduce the heat, cover, and simmer 10 minutes. Add the noodles, and return to a boil. Cook until the noodles are tender, 8 to 10 minutes. Stir in the fish. Simmer for 1 minute.

MAKES 4 TO 6 SERVINGS.

Turtle Soup

I don't know where on earth I came up with this turtle soup recipe. I believe a butcher in Donelson gave it to me many years ago when I did a story about his catching turtles out of Stones River. I do recall his telling me how delicious turtle soup can be. I was told this recipe is something like 140 years old. By the way, this guy caught turtles that were huge—2½ to 3 feet across the backs of their shells. —JIMMY

3   **pounds turtle meat**

4   **quarts water**

3   **tablespoons all-purpose flour**

2   **tablespoons shortening**

2   **medium onions, chopped**

3   **sticks celery, minced**

6   **cloves garlic, minced**

1   **large green pepper, minced**

2   **lemons, thinly sliced**

4   **tablespoons Worcestershire sauce**

     Tony Chachere's Creole Seasoning Salt

     McCormick's Season Salt

3   **heaping tablespoons whole allspice, tied in a thin cloth**

1   **tablespoon sherry per serving**

4   **hard-cooked eggs**

     Parsley

Boil the turtle meat in the water until tender. Remove the scum with a spoon. Make a roux with the shortening and flour. Add the onions, celery, garlic, and green pepper. Remove the turtle meat from the stock, strain the stock, and add the roux to the stock. Bones may be removed from the turtle meat. Add the meat to the stock along with the lemons, Worcestershire sauce, and seasoning salts to taste. Place the bag of allspice in the soup, and simmer for one hour. Add 1 tablespoon sherry to each serving, if desired. Garnish with the sliced, hard-cooked eggs, and the parsley.

MAKES 4 TO 6 SERVINGS.

Dutch Oven Turtle Soup

Meat from a 5- to 8-pound alligator, snapping, or softshell turtle

Bacon drippings

6 **large potatoes**

1 **onion**

1 **(1-pound) bag carrots**

1 **(16-ounce) can corn**

1 **(14-ounce) can beef or chicken stock**

Cut the turtle meat into ½-inch cubes. Brown the meat in the bacon drippings. Cut the veggies into large chunks. Put all the turtle meat, potatoes, onion, carrots, corn, and beef or chicken stock in a Dutch oven, and cover with water. Bury the Dutch oven in a fire pit under coals. Go fishing. After 8 hours, dig out the pot, and dig in.

MAKES 4 TO 6 SERVINGS.

Easy as Duck Soup

Kevin "Bowana" Moore
Nashville, Tennessee

2 **duck carcasses**

3 **onions, chopped**

3 **carrots, chopped**

1 **rib celery, chopped**

6 **pints water**

Bouquet garni

Salt and pepper

4 **ounces red wine**

Chopped parsley for garnish

Preheat the oven to 450 degrees. Remove all the skin and fat from the carcasses, and reserve. Chop the carcasses into small pieces, and put them into a roasting pan with 2 of the onions, the carrots, and celery. Place in the oven, and cook for 30 minutes, turning occasionally until brown all over. Remove the carcasses to a stockpot. Add the cold water, the bouquet garni, salt, and pepper. Add the red wine to the roasting pan, and stir over medium heat to loosen the sediment; add it to the stock pot. Bring the mixture to a boil, skim away any foam, and simmer for 4 to 5 hours, skimming the surface occasionally. Strain the stock into a fresh pot, and reduce it to 1½ pints. Cool and remove all fat. Add the remaining chopped vegetables, and cook for 30 minutes. Sprinkle with chopped parsley and serve.

MAKES 10 TO 12 SERVINGS.

Pheasant Soup

David Fast
Lexington, Kentucky

3	**pheasant carcasses**
	Oil
½	**cup coarsely chopped onion**
½	**cup coarsely chopped carrots**
½	**cup coarsely chopped celery**
	Seasonings
	Noodles, rice, barley, vegetables, or potatoes
	Cornstarch (optional)

Place the carcasses in a large stockpot with a small amount of cooking oil and the onions, carrots, and celery. Brown thoroughly on high heat until the vegetables begin to caramelize and the meat is well done. (Undercooking will cause cloudy stock from blood cooked out of the meat into the stock.) The dark color of the caramelized vegetables makes a rich, dark stock, about the color of tea. Add water to cover, and simmer until the meat can be easily removed from the bones. Take the bones out of the stock, and strain the stock to remove the remaining vegetables and scraps. Season to taste. Remove the meat from the bones, and reserve for the soup. If desired, add a small amount of cornstarch dissolved in water to give body to the stock. Cook noodles, rice, wild rice, barley, vegetables, or potatoes in the stock. Add the meat at the last minute; heat through.

SERVINGS WILL DEPEND ON THE AMOUNT OF MEAT AND VEGETABLES.

You might be inclined to think that the bigger the pattern, the better, but this is not necessarily so. If your pattern is too wide at your target range, there will not be enough shot on the target to do the job.

Venison Soup

Fred Scarbrough
Murfreesboro, Tennessee

½	**pound venison**
1	**onion**
2	**carrots, sliced**
3	**ribs celery**
6	**pods okra**
1	**(15-ounce) can whole kernel corn**
1	**(15-ounce) can English peas**
4	**potatoes, peeled and diced**
2	**quarts tomatoes**
	Salt and pepper

Put the venison in a soup pot, and cover with water; cook until tender. Take the meat out of the pan and chop. Dice the onion, carrots, and celery, and add to the pot along with the chopped venison. Cook until onion, carrots, and celery are tender. Then add the okra, corn, peas, and potatoes to the pot, and cook until potatoes are done. Add tomatoes and bring to a boil. Add salt and pepper to taste.

MAKES 4 SERVINGS.

Onion Soup

½	**pound white onions, sliced**
¼	**cup butter**
2	**tablespoons corn oil**
3	**tablespoons all-purpose flour**
1	**quart chicken broth**
1	**quart beef broth**
8	**slices French bread**
	Shredded Swiss cheese
	Grated Parmesan

Sauté the onions in butter and oil until onions are transparent, but not browned. When tender, turn the heat to the lowest point, and sprinkle the onions with flour, stirring vigorously. Pour into a Dutch oven, and stir in the broths. Heat thoroughly, and divide among 8 ovenproof bowls. Float a slice of the bread atop each serving. Mix equal parts of the Swiss and the Parmesan cheese to a smooth paste and spread over the bread. Preheat the oven to broil. Place all the bowls on an oven rack 4 inches from the broiler, and broil until the cheese melts. Serve at once.

MAKES 8 SERVINGS.

Expeditious Potato Soup

1½ cups peeled, grated potato

2 tablespoons grated onion

1 (11-ounce) can evaporated milk

2 cups milk

¼ cup water

2 tablespoons all-purpose flour

Salt and pepper

2 tablespoons fresh parsley

Place the potatoes and onions in a saucepan, and cover with water. Bring the water to a boil, reduce the heat to medium, and simmer until the potatoes are done. Do not drain. Add the evaporated milk and the regular milk. Continue cooking and stirring until the mixture is hot. Combine the water and flour, and mix until blended. Add to the potato mixture, stirring until mixture thickens. Add the salt and pepper to taste. Stir in the parsley.

MAKES 4 SERVINGS.

Simple Corn Chowder

2 medium potatoes

1 medium onion

2 cups water

1 (16-ounce) can creamed corn

1 (10-ounce) can niblets corn

Butter

1 cup milk

Salt and pepper

In a saucepan, cook the potatoes and onion in boiling water. Once cooked, do not drain the cooking liquid; add the cans of corn. Add the milk and salt and pepper to taste. Continue heating until hot. Put a pat of butter in the soup bowl, and ladle in the hot soup.

MAKES 4 SERVINGS.

Vegetable and Cheese Chowder

$\frac{1}{3}$ cup uncooked quick or old-fashioned oats

1 cup sliced celery

$\frac{1}{2}$ cup chopped onion

2 tablespoons butter

2 cups milk

2 cups water

1 (16-ounce) package frozen mixed vegetables

1 teaspoon mustard

$\frac{1}{2}$ teaspoon salt

$\frac{1}{8}$ teaspoon black pepper

2 cups (or 8 ounces) shredded cheddar cheese

Place the oats in a food processor or blender, cover, and process for 1 minute. In a 4-quart saucepan or a Dutch oven, sauté the celery and onion in the butter until tender. Blend in the ground oats. Gradually add the milk and water. Continue cooking over medium heat, stirring constantly, until thickened. Reduce the heat. Add the vegetables, mustard, salt, and pepper. Continue cooking over low heat for 10 minutes, or until the vegetables are heated through. Remove from the heat, add the cheese, and stir until well blended.

MAKES 4 TO 6 SERVINGS.

Note:

For the frozen vegetables, you can substitute canned or fresh vegetables of your choice, but you will need to cut the cooking time down a bit.

New England Clam Chowder

Cathy Summerlin
Leipers Fork, Tennessee

2 (6-ounce) cans chopped clams

2 (10$\frac{1}{2}$-ounce) cans condensed potato soup

1 cup half-and-half

1 medium onion, finely diced

2 garlic cloves, finely diced

Drain 1 can of the clams, but save the liquid from the remaining can. Mix the potato soup, clams with liquid, half-and-half, onion, and garlic into a medium saucepan, and bring to a boil over medium heat, stirring constantly for 10 to 15 minutes. Reduce the heat to low, and simmer for an additional 10 minutes.

MAKES 4 SERVINGS.

Beer Cheese Soup

Mrs. Stan Winkleman
Nashville, Tennessee

8   cups milk

2   teaspoons Tabasco

4   teaspoons Worcestershire
     sauce

4   tablespoons chicken base

16   ounces Cheez Whiz

6   tablespoons cornstarch

⅓   cup water

1   cup beer

     Cayenne

Combine the milk, Tabasco, Worcestershire sauce, and chicken base. Bring to a boil, stirring regularly. Add the Cheez Whiz, after warming the jar in hot water or in the microwave. Mix in well. Dissolve the cornstarch completely in the water. Add to the soup, which should thicken immediately. Reduce the heat a bit, and stir in the beer. To serve, ladle into bowls, and dust with the cayenne.

MAKES 6 SERVINGS.

When fishing for bluegill, thin-diameter lines are best. I use 4-pound test most of the time. I prefer the clear-finish line. If the bluegill are skittish, try 2-pound test line. Try garden worms, red wigglers, crickets, and shrimp, plus lures such as grubs, spinnerbaits, plastic insect imitations, and spinners.

Chapter 12

Desserts

Since sugar came into common use, nothing has been so popular at the table as desserts. Many Tennessee households wouldn't think supper complete without a slice of pie, a piece of cake, or a handful of cookies. Desserts are simply a fine Southern tradition.

Bread Pudding

Bobbie McAllister
Johnson City, Tennessee

10	**slices bread**
3	**cups skim milk**
1½ cups sugar	
1	**cup egg substitute**
4	**tablespoons diet margarine**
2	**teaspoons vanilla**
1	**cup crushed pineapple**

Preheat the oven to 350 degrees. Break the bread into pieces in a 9 x 13-inch baking dish. Blend in half the milk. Add the sugar and egg substitute, mixing well after each. Dice the margarine on top, and stir in the vanilla, remaining milk, and pineapple. Bake for 40 minutes, until firm.

MAKES 6 TO 8 SERVINGS.

Persimmon Pudding

Kingston Springs, Tennessee

If the pudding falls a little, so much the better. And if it seems soggy, that's also for the better.
—SHARON BENEFIELD

1   pint buttermilk

1   pint ripe persimmons

1   cup sugar

1   egg

1   tablespoon butter

½   teaspoon baking powder

½   teaspoon baking soda

¼   teaspoon cloves

½   teaspoon allspice

1   teaspoon cinnamon
     Flour for a thin batter
     Topping (recipe follows)

Preheat the oven to 350 degrees. Mix the buttermilk with the persimmons. Press through a sieve or colander, and add the sugar, egg, butter, baking powder, baking soda, cloves, allspice, and cinnamon. Add enough flour to make a stiff batter, but not so stiff as cake dough. Bake in a square pan at 350 degrees, until done. When you are ready to serve, cut the pudding into squares. Place the squares on a broiler pan and spoon the topping over the squares. Turn the oven to broil, and place the squares under the broiler; cook until bubbly.

MAKES 6 TO 8 SERVINGS.

Topping

½   cup sugar

¼   cup milk

½   teaspoon cinnamon

1   tablespoon flour

1   tablespoon butter

Mix the sugar, milk, cinnamon, and flour. Bring to a boil. Add the butter and mix.

Chocolate Chess Pie

Debbie White

½   **stick margarine**

3   **tablespoons cocoa**

1½ **cups sugar**

½   **cup chopped pecans**

1   **teaspoon flour**

2   **eggs, slightly beaten**

1   **teaspoon vanilla**

½   **cup evaporated milk**

1   **9-inch piecrust, unbaked**

Preheat the oven to 400 degrees. Melt the margarine. Add the cocoa, sugar, pecans, flour, eggs, vanilla, and evaporated milk, and mix thoroughly. Pour into the piecrust. Bake in the oven for 10 minutes. Reduce the oven temperature to 325 degrees, and bake for 30 minutes more.

MAKES 8 SERVINGS.

Tennessee Hillbilly Lemon Chess Pie

Judy and Phillip Russell
Pulaski, Tennessee

2   **cups sugar**

1   **tablespoon flour**

1   **tablespoon cornmeal**

¼   **teaspoon salt**

¼   **cup melted butter or margarine**

¼   **cup lemon juice**

    Grated rinds of 2 lemons

¼   **cup milk**

4   **eggs**

1   **9-inch piecrust, unbaked**

Preheat the oven to 350 degrees. Combine the sugar, flour, cornmeal, and salt. Add the butter, lemon juice, lemon rinds, and milk. Blend well. Add the eggs, beating well. Pour into the piecrust. Bake in the oven for 50 minutes.

MAKES 8 SERVINGS.

Chess Fruit Pie

Annie Collier
Grady, Alabama

1 cup brown sugar

½ cup margarine

½ cup cream

3 whole eggs plus
   1 egg yolk

1 cup chopped English
   walnuts

1 cup raisins

1 teaspoon vanilla

1 teaspoon lemon rind

1 teaspoon lemon juice

2 tablespoons white sugar

1 egg white, stiffly beaten

1 9-inch piecrust, unbaked
   Whipping cream

Preheat the oven to 350 degrees. Cream the sugar and margarine. Add the cream, and mix well. Add the eggs and yolk, one at a time, beating well after each addition. Add the nuts, raisins, vanilla, lemon rind, and lemon juice. Mix well. Beat the white sugar into the stiffly beaten egg white, and fold into the pie mixture. Pour into the piecrust, and bake in the oven for 40 minutes or until set. Serve with a dollop of whipped cream.

MAKES 8 SERVINGS.

Impossible Coconut Pie

Auda Eldridge
Nashville, Tennessee

2 eggs, beaten

1 cup milk

½ teaspoon vanilla

¼ stick butter or margarine

1 cup sugar

¼ cup self-rising flour

1 (3½-ounce) package flaked
   coconut

Preheat the oven to 350 degrees. Beat the eggs. Blend in the milk, vanilla, butter, sugar, flour, and coconut. Turn into a greased 9-inch pie pan. Bake in the oven for 30 minutes. The pie makes its own crust.

MAKES 8 SERVINGS.

Granny's Egg Custard Pie

Auda Eldridge
Nashville, Tennessee

3	eggs
1	cup sugar
½	teaspoon salt
½	teaspoon vanilla extract
½	teaspoon nutmeg
1	pint milk
1	9-inch piecrust, unbaked

Preheat the oven to 325 degrees. Beat the eggs, and add the sugar, salt, vanilla, and nutmeg. Add the scalded milk (not boiled), and mix. Pour into the piecrust, and bake in the oven for 50 minutes, or until a knife blade comes out clean.

MAKES 8 SERVINGS.

Apricot Nectar Cake

Auda Eldridge
Nashville, Tennessee

4	eggs
1	cup apricot nectar
¾	cup oil
1	box Lemon Supreme cake mix
	Icing (recipe follows)

Preheat the oven to 350 degrees. Beat the eggs, apricot nectar, and oil. Add the cake mix and beat. Pour into a deep cake pan and bake in the oven for 40 minutes. Cool the cake and drizzle the icing over it.

MAKES 8 SERVINGS.

Icing

1	cup powdered sugar
3	tablespoons lemon juice

In a small bowl mix the sugar and lemon juice.

Pecan Bars

Annie Collier
Grady, Alabama

2 cups all-purpose flour

½ cup sugar

⅛ teaspoon salt

¾ cup (1½ sticks) butter or margarine, plus ½ cup

1 cup firmly packed brown sugar

1 cup light corn syrup

4 large eggs, lightly beaten

2½ cups finely chopped pecans

1 teaspoon vanilla extract

Preheat the oven to 350 degrees. Combine the flour, sugar, and salt in a large bowl, and cut in the ¾ cup butter with a pastry blender until the mixture resembles very fine crumbs. Press the mixture evenly into a greased 13 x 9-inch pan, using a piece of plastic wrap to press the crumb mixture firmly in the pan. Bake in the oven for 17 to 20 minutes, or until lightly browned. Combine the brown sugar, corn syrup, and the ½ cup butter in a saucepan, and bring to a boil over medium heat, stirring gently. Remove from the heat. Stir ¼ of the hot mixture into the beaten eggs, and then add to the remaining hot mixture. Stir in the pecans and vanilla. Pour the filling over the crust. Bake in the oven for 35 minutes, or until set. Cool completely in the pan on a wire rack. Cut into bars.

MAKES 28 TO 30 (2-INCH SQUARE) BARS.

Frozen Salad or Dessert

Debbie White

1   (8-ounce) package cream cheese, softened

1   (8-ounce) bowl refrigerated whipped topping

1   (10-ounce) package strawberries

1   cup chopped pecans or walnuts

1   (20-ounce) can crushed pineapple, with juice

¾   cup sugar

3   bananas

Mix the cream cheese well with the whipped topping; add the strawberries, nuts, pineapple, sugar, and bananas. Pour into a freezer container, and freeze. The dessert will keep for several weeks.

MAKES 6 TO 8 SERVINGS.

Index